2nd Edition

The Complete Guide to

Real Estate Cash Flow Analysis

How to Analyze Any Investment Property for Greater Profits with Less Risk

Douglas K. Rutherford, CPA

Copyright © 2007-2008 by Douglas K. Rutherford. All rights reserved. Printed in the United States of America. Except as permitted under the United States Copyright Act of 1976, no part of this publication may be reproduced or distributed in any form or by any means, or stored in a database or retrieval system, without the prior written permission of the publisher.

ISBN 978-1-59872-900-9

Published by:
Instantpublisher.com
a division of
Fundcraft Publishing Company
Collierville TN 38027

This publication is designed to provide accurate and authoritative information relating to the subject matter covered. It is sold with the understanding that the author and publisher are not engaged in rendering legal, accounting, or other professional advice. If legal advice or other expert assistance is required, the services of a competent person should be sought.

Dedication

This book is dedicated to all of you who have always wanted to invest in real estate but have lacked the confidence, knowledge, and necessary tools to buy your first property. I hope the information in this book and the Cash Flow Analyzer® software will be the tools that will help you get out of your comfort zone and finally make the plunge.

I also dedicate this book to my lovely wife, Denise, who provides me unconditional love and support everyday and throughout our twenty-two years of marriage, and to my two beautiful daughters, Laurel and Madelyn, who gave up a lot of daddy-time so I could finish this book.

Preface

Over the past fifteen years, since we first introduced the Cash Flow Analyzer® software to the public, my staff and I have spoken to tens of thousands of real estate investors, agents, brokers, and investor wannabes at tradeshows, at REIA meetings, and on the telephone. We hear many of the same questions and see the same mistakes being made by investors throughout the country.

The purpose of this book is to help clear up some of the confusion that exists in the world of real estate finance, a world filled with hundreds of financial ratios, thousands of terms, and a million different ways of evaluating investment properties. This unnecessary confusion has led to poor investment choices by many investors or, even worse, complete decision-making paralysis. This book is designed to be used in conjunction with the Cash Flow Analyzer® software and is intended to focus on the main factors that help real estate investors make **quicker and better real estate investment decisions with less risk**.

Plenty of books and other resources are on the market that can barrage you with page upon confusing page of how to calculate financial ratios. Since the purpose of this book is not to add to the confusion, I will simply explain the terms and ratios in a manner that is easily understood, and we will let the Cash Flow Analyzer® software do the number crunching for us. In addition, I will teach you which ratios in the Cash Flow Analyzer® are most pertinent depending on the investment scenario, and I will discuss other important factors to consider before purchasing a property.

Table of Contents

Preface 4

Introduction

The Real Estate Investing Frenzy 7

Section I: Real Estate Concepts

1. Real Estate Investing: Making Money vs. Building Wealth 8

2. Three Cornerstones of Real Estate Wealth 10
    I. Cash Flow 11
    II. Equity from Loan Payments 12
    III. Appreciation 13

3. Understanding the Decision-Making Matrix 16
    I. Risk 17
    II. Return-on-Investment (ROI) 20
    III. Time and Effort 23

4. Leveraging 25

5. Flipping vs. Speculating and Mortgage Fraud 27

Section II: Cash Fow Analysis

6. Starting the Analysis Process 30

7. Landlord's Cash Flow Analyzer® Software 32
    I. Rental Income and Expenses 32
    II. Property Costs and Characteristics 35
    III. Financing 38
    IV. Income Taxes 39

Section III: Financial Ratios and Terms

8. Net Operating Income (NOI) 45

9. Present Value (PV) and Net Present Value (NPV) 47

10. Internal Rate of Return (IRR) 51

11. Modified Internal Rate of Return (MIRR) 52

12. Debt Coverage Ratio (DCR) 53

13. Cash-on-Cash Return 54

14. Cash-on-Cash Return with Equity Build-Up 56

15. Capitalization Rate (Cap Rate) 58

16. Loan-to-Value Ratio (LVR) 60

17. Gross Rent Multiplier (GRM) 61

Section IV: Sample Analysis

18. Sample Analysis #1 62

19. Sample Analysis #2 67

20. Sample Analysis #3 70

21. Sample Analysis #4 74

Section V: Real Estate Term Glossary

Section VI: Appendices

Appendix 1: Input Data Sheets and Other Reports for Sample Analysis #1 99

Appendix 2: Input Data Sheet for Sample Analysis #2 109

Appendix 3: Input Data Sheet for Sample Analysis #3 110

Appendix 4: Input Data Sheet for Sample Analysis #4 111

Appendix 5 - 2007 Individual Tax Tables 115

Introduction

The Real Estate Investing Frenzy

Throughout the ages, people have traveled far and wide to jump on the latest get-rich-quick "money-making" bandwagon. We have all seen those late-night infomercials paid for by supposed real estate multi-millionaires promising the road to riches *"for just three easy payments of $29.95."* With *"just a few hours a week and no money down,"* in no time at all, you can be a multi-millionaire, too!

Anyone who tells you that you are going to get rich quick and easy is not being honest with you. Don't get me wrong, there are many legitimate strategies for making money and creating wealth in real estate; but they require time, effort, and usually money. For every strategy there are probably twenty real estate "gurus" who want to sell you a real estate course. I personally know many of them, and I put them into two categories: those who should be charging twice as much as they do because of the value they offer and those who, quite frankly, should be sentenced to personally implement their own strategies. Be mindful of who is giving you advice. You don't always get what you pay for.

With that said, these "gurus" want to teach you *"how"* to obtain properties and, maybe, *"what"* to do once you have obtained them. Of course, the *"how's"* and *"what's"* are extremely important, but they do not address *"if"* you should buy the property in the first place.

Obviously, not all properties are suitable for investment purposes. The *"if"* is what this book, along with the Cash Flow Analyzer® Software, addresses. If you want to make money and build wealth through real estate, you have to learn how to select the right properties. If you invest wisely and for the long-haul, you have placed yourself on one of the surest paths to wealth and financial freedom.

Section 1: Real Estate Concepts

Chapter 1

Real Estate Investing: Making Money vs. Building Wealth

So what is the difference between making money and building wealth? Although many people confuse the two, making money and becoming wealthy are two very different things. The difference is probably best explained by way of example.

George vs. John

Let's take a look at George, an attorney making $350,000 a year. He spends most of his income to cover the mortgage on an expensive home, luxurious vacations, and a fancy car. Even though his friends are impressed with his high-profile job, palatial mansion, and European sports car, George is broke! George's net worth (assets minus liabilities) is zero, and he has no investments or assets generating income. He is simply living hand-to-mouth. If George wants to eat next week, he will have to go to work and sue someone on behalf of a client. George looks like a million bucks, but on paper he's little different than a welfare recipient. And in actuality, if things were to turn unfavorably for George, he could easily become one.

John, on the other hand, is a school teacher making $45,000 a year. He lives in a modest house and drives a 1995 Ford pickup. Over the years, John has bought ten rental properties with very little of his own money. The debts on these properties have been paid off through the rents collected from his tenants, and his properties have continued to appreciate over the years. John is sitting on over $1,000,000 of equity that is generating an additional $75,000 a year of cash flow whether he gets out of bed in the morning or not. John does not look or act like a millionaire, but he is. John builds wealth. George makes money. John buys assets. George buys liabilities he *thinks* are assets. If you understand this concept, you understand the key to building wealth in real estate.

If you have not done so, I highly recommend that you read the book *The Millionaire Next Door* by Thomas J. Stanley and William D. Danko. This book will forever change your thinking regarding who the rich really are and how they obtained their wealth. I also highly recommend the book *RichDad PoorDad* by Robert Kiyosaki. This book will explain why changing your mindset from that of an employee to that of an entrepreneur is the path to wealth.

Chapter 2

Three Cornerstones of Real Estate Wealth

As I mentioned earlier, there are many strategies for making money in real estate, e.g. flipping, renting, short sales, and wholesaling. Regardless of which strategy you decide to implement, at least one of the three following elements is required to make money and build wealth. I refer to these three elements as the **Three Cornerstones of Real Estate Wealth**:

- Cash Flow
- Equity from Loan Payments
- Appreciation

Three Cornerstones of Wealth Building Through Real Estate Investing

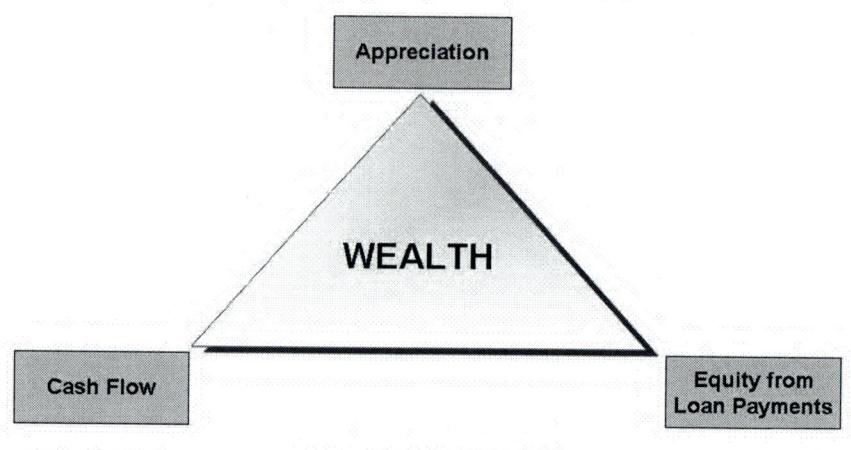

```
            Appreciation
               /\
              /  \
             /    \
            / WEALTH\
           /         \
          /_____\
      Cash Flow    Equity from
                   Loan Payments
```

© 2007 LandlordSoftware.com LLC

① Cash Flow — 1st cornerstone to building wealth

The first of the three cornerstones of wealth building is **cash flow**. Simply stated, cash flow is the money left over after all expenses, such as property taxes, mortgage payments, and income taxes have been paid. If the income (rent, parking fees, late fees, etc.) is sufficient to cover all of the expenses, the property has what we call a positive cash flow. Not every real estate investment will have a positive cash flow, by either design (because of the type of real estate strategy) or poor planning.

The annual cash flow of a property is calculated as follows:

> Gross Annual Rental Income
> − Annual Operating Expenses
> − Annual Loan Payments
> − Annual Income Taxes
>
> **Annual Cash Flow**

2 most important factors for +CF

The two most important factors in determining if a property will have a positive cash flow is the ***amount you pay*** for the property (including costs of putting the property in rentable condition) and the ***amount of rent*** you collect. Generally, the better the property's condition, the better the chance of finding a tenant and obtaining the highest possible rent.

mm/n mistakes

Receiving a positive cash flow from a rental property is, of course, easier said than done. Investors must maintain a balance between the amount of collectible rent and the cost of the property and its upkeep. Common mistakes made by investors include spending too much for a property or putting too much money into upgrades (e.g. granite countertops) when rents cannot be increased enough to justify these expenditures. Of course, other expenses (e.g. property taxes, insurance, and repairs) need to be managed as well.

The Most Rent for the Least Cost

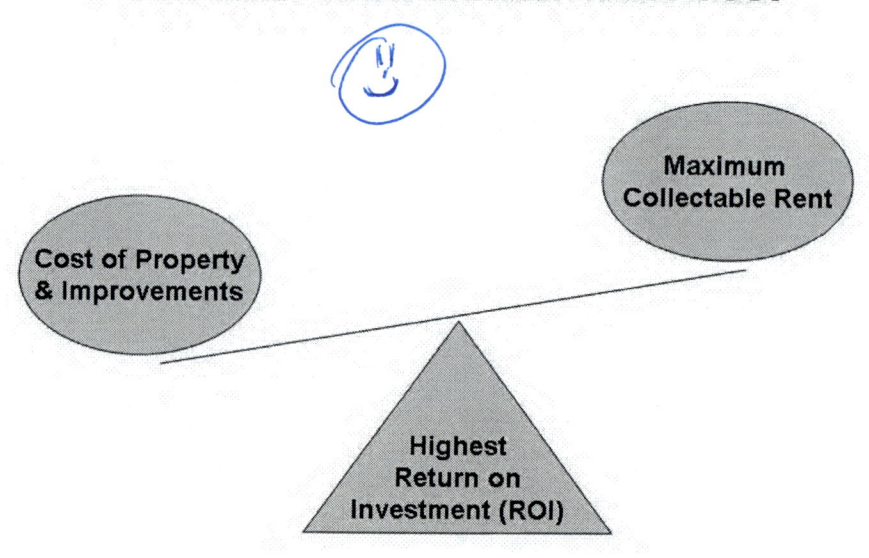

(Diagram: a balance/seesaw with "Cost of Property & Improvements" on the left, "Maximum Collectable Rent" on the right, and "Highest Return on Investment (ROI)" as the fulcrum triangle.)

② Equity from Loan Payments — 2nd Cornerstone to Building Wealth

The second cornerstone to building wealth in real estate is **equity from loan payments.** This type of equity is created as principal payments are made on the loan, which generally translates into future cash flow when the property is sold. This wealth is created by having the tenant pay you enough rent to cover the mortgage payments and other costs; in other words having the tenant pay off the mortgage for you.

The equity from loan payments is calculated as follows:

      Cost of the Property
— Current Loan Balance

      Equity from Loan Payments

Appreciation – 3rd Cornerstone to Building Wealth

Last, but by no means least, the third and most significant way of building wealth in real estate is through **appreciation**. Appreciation is generally defined as the increase in the value of a particular property over its original cost (of course, real estate can also *depreciate* or decrease in value as well.) Some of the factors that affect a property's rate of appreciation or depreciation are the following:

- Location
- Inflation / Deflation
- Market conditions (e.g. supply and demand)
- Local economy
- Demographics
- Zoning (highest and best use)
- Cash flow
- Property condition

(Affect Rate of Appreciation / Depreciation)

Understanding how these factors affect the value of a property is critical when deciding whether to buy, hold, or sell a property. For more information, check your local library for books on real estate investing.

You have probably heard the old adage, when purchasing real estate, the three most important things to consider are **location, location, location**. This statement couldn't be more true, because the single biggest factor affecting the appreciation of a property is its location. In fact, the location of a property has a direct impact on virtually all other factors that affect the value of a property, e.g. supply, demand, and zoning.

The value of a property is made up of two components: the value of the land and the value of any improvements made to the land (e.g. house, office building, or parking lot). The ratio of the value of the land compared to the value of the improvements is called the land-to-improvements ratio. This ratio can change drastically depending on the location of a property.

The value of land will almost always go up over time, primarily because, as Mark Twain so eloquently put it, "... they're not making it anymore." In addition, land never wears out. Improvements, on the other hand, will generally depreciate due to such things as wear and tear, better construction methods, and trends. The goal is to purchase properties where the value of the land will increase to more than offset the depreciation of the improvements.

> **Example:** Assume you purchased a rental property thirty years ago in a great location. The value of the land most likely would have appreciated more that the depreciation of the actual structure. In other words, even though the house has a harvest gold and avocado colored kitchen, the increase in land value could justify upgrading the property with newer cabinets and appliances.

This is why when I purchase investment properties, I select properties within a fifteen-minute driving time to a thriving economic center. These properties tend to have a higher land-to-improvement ratio. A thorough discussion of these factors is beyond the scope of this book. I highly recommend *The Unofficial Guide to Real Estate Investing* by Spencer Strauss and Martin Stone for a more thorough explanation of the factors affecting the appreciation of a property.

Commercial vs. Residential

When you invest in other than single-family houses, such as apartment buildings, duplexes, commercial properties, or even subsidized housing, the value of the property is defined more by its cash flow and return-on-investment than anything else. Thus, the appreciation on such property is defined by its projected increase in cash flow.

For example, let's take a single-family property with a view of the San Francisco Bay. The value of this property is defined more by its location than its cash flow. Thus, the appreciation on this property is connected more to its location and the overall local market condition.

The monthly mortgage on the above property will probably always exceed what rents you could collect. Even though this property would have a negative cash flow, the value of the property is defined by the fact that someone would be willing to purchase the property for other than investment purposes. Of course, an investor would only buy this property if he believed that the appreciation on the property would be enough to cover the years of negative cash flow and have enough left over to deliver an appropriate rate-of-return.

Now let's assume that the property is a multi-unit apartment building around the corner. Ms. Jones would probably never want to purchase this property to live in no matter how gorgeous the view. So, therefore, the only buyer that would be interested in this property would be another investor. So how does an investor value this property? An investor values the property based on the projected rate-of-return, which is mostly made up of the property's annual cash flow.

An investor only purchases a multi-unit apartment building for its cash flow; therefore, its cash flow determines the value. Thus the future "appreciation" on this property will be a function of its future increase in cash flow. When projecting the future appreciation of a commercial or multi-family complex, determining the factors that affect cash flow (e.g. rental income and expenses) are important.

15

Chapter 3

Understanding the Decision-Making Matrix

Now that we have discussed the three cornerstones that contribute to wealth building, let's discuss the actual decision-making process. The decision of whether or not to invest in a particular property is based on three factors: **risk**, **time and effort**, and **return-on-investment**. Ignoring any one of the factors can be *hazardous to your wealth*.

Decision-Making Matrix

No ROI, No T&E, High Risk

No ROI, Average T&E, Average Risk

Average ROI, Average T&E, High Risk

Time & Effort (T&E)

Avoid | Avoid

BUY!

Risk | Maybe | **Return on Investment (ROI)**

No ROI, High T&E, No Risk

High ROI, High T&E, High Risk

Average ROI, High T&E, Average Risk

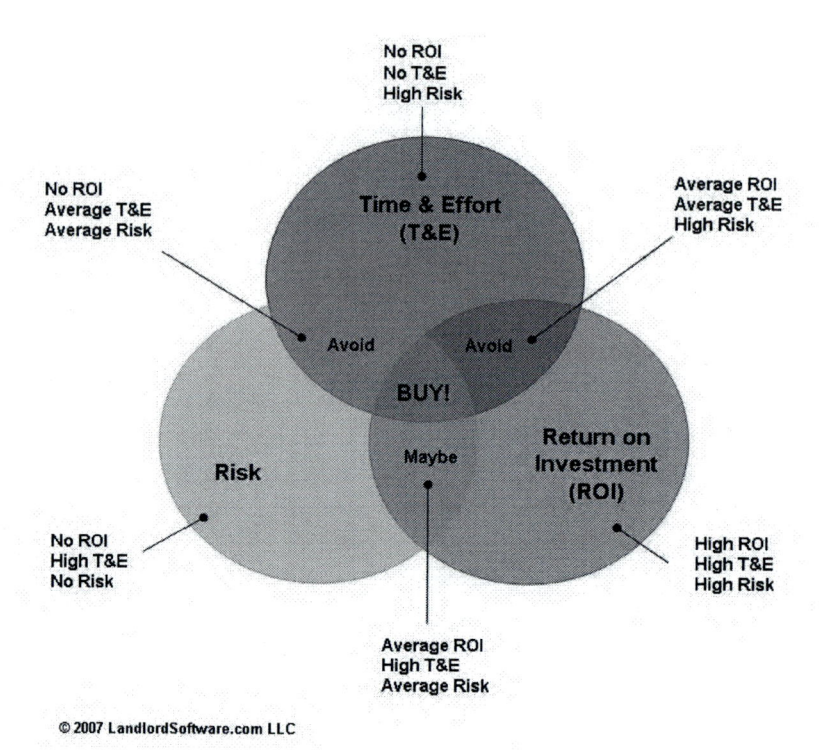

© 2007 LandlordSoftware.com LLC

Risk

Historically, real estate has proven to be one of the safest investments; however, like nearly all investments, there is a risk component that must be addressed. Assessing risk is an integral part of doing your homework *before* purchasing each and every property.

Risks vary based on the type of property and investment strategy. The key to assessing risk is to identify, quantify, and then mitigate the risks, if possible. Some examples of risk include fire, lawsuits, hidden termite damage, and title disputes. Measures to mitigate these risks include purchasing property and casualty insurance, using limited liability companies, getting thorough property inspections, and purchasing title insurance.

The types of risks also vary depending on the location of the property. For example, the laws in some states are so skewed in favor of tenants that landlords have to go through a long and arduous eviction process, sometimes taking up to twelve months to evict a tenant. Could you afford to go an entire year without receiving rent? Other risks associated with the location include the length of time it may take you to find a viable tenant, the number of days it will take to sell a property, and even the possibility of theft.

When making a decision to purchase a property, carefully assess the risks. Generally, the more risk you take, the greater the return-on-investment needs to be to compensate you for the risk you are taking. Conversely, a lower risk means you can accept a lower return-on-investment.

Although most risks can be readily identified, many are unforeseen. Let me share with you several unforeseen risks that my wife and I have encountered.

- My wife's very first real estate purchase was a fixer-upper on a lush one-acre lot with a beautiful meandering brook. She was thrilled with her find and quite proud of her real estate savvy, until the following spring. During a period of heavy rain, the quiet little brook turned into a raging river, and the house became encircled by a moat! Since the house had been there for over fifty years, it never occurred to her to check the flood-zone maps.

- I once purchased an ugly house with aluminum siding for the purpose of doing a quick flip and earning some fast cash. My plans were to have the siding replaced with hardy-plank, paint the house, and place it back on the market. Even though I paid an experienced home inspector to check out the property prior to my purchase, when the old dented siding was removed, I had two unforeseen problems. First, most of the old house was covered with asbestos siding, which I now had to disclose to potential buyers. Secondly, concealed between the sheetrock and siding was so much termite damage that nearly half of the exterior walls had to be replaced. What I thought was a low-risk, low-time-and-effort, high-return investment quickly turned into a high-risk, high-time-and-effort, low-return investment.

- Another surprise came when I purchased a property that was in foreclosure due to the death of the homeowner. I later learned from the next-door neighbor that the homeowner had committed suicide after a long bout with AIDS. Even though I had completely gutted the house and replaced all the plumbing, walls, floors, ceilings, windows, and doors, that neighbor still felt it was her responsibility to inform potential tenants of the "situation." Every time a prospective tenant got near the house, she showed up to share the gory details. Naturally, this situation played havoc with my vacancy-rate assumption.

- One month after I purchased a house, a registered sex-offender moved in across the street. I became aware of the situation only after a buyer withdrew his offer. The local real estate agency, wishing to limit its liability in such cases, had inserted a sex-offender clause into the purchase agreement requiring clients to check the state sex-offender registry before signing.

- Due to the recent surge in the price of copper, not one but **two** of my properties have had the copper pipes stolen from under the houses. The thief, who received only a few dollars from the salvage yard, left me with thousands of dollars of plumbing damage.

Fortunately, not all unforeseen events are negative. Here are a couple of more encouraging examples:

- Last year, I purchased a property adjacent to an unsightly detention pond. I was unaware (and fortunately so was the bank) that the county had plans to invest $2 million into a beautification project to turn the detention pond into a lake surrounded by a park with jogging trails, park benches, and landscaping. Six months later, I sold the house and netted nearly $50,000 more that my original cash-flow projection.

- Another unforeseen windfall came when Wal-Mart tore down an abandoned shopping center down the street from one of my properties and built a brand new Super Center. My vacancy rate on this property has gone to nearly zero, and my cash flow has increased significantly due to this unforeseen event.

Return-on-Investment (ROI)

You hear the term **return-on-investment** used all the time and you know it is important, but what does it mean? How do you calculate return-on-investment? OK, that was a trick question. Return-on-investment is a general or umbrella term used to define many different methods of calculating return, not a specific method. For example, two of the many ways to compute a return-on-investment are cash-on-cash and internal-rate-of-return (IRR). These two methods, along with other calculations, are defined in the Financial Ratio section of this book.

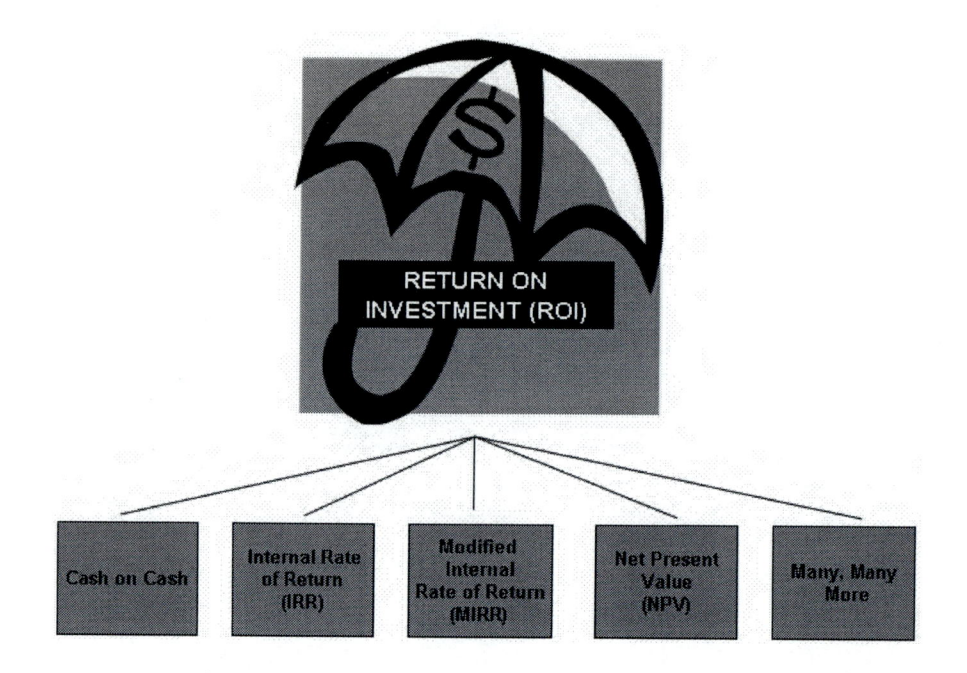

RETURN ON INVESTMENT (ROI)

- Cash on Cash
- Internal Rate of Return (IRR)
- Modified Internal Rate of Return (MIRR)
- Net Present Value (NPV)
- Many, Many More

The term return-on-investment is much like the term "payment." Someone may agree to pay you, but payment could be in the form of cash, check, credit card, stock, cash-over-time, or labor. So the term "payment" does not mean "cash." Payment is an umbrella term covering various forms of payment.

The same confusion is made with the term return-on-investment. If I were to offer you an investment with a guaranteed 40% return, would you be interested? Would you invest $10,000 with me if I guaranteed to pay you back your $10,000 plus $4,000 (i.e. 40%) of earnings?

What if I told you it would be ten years before you received the $14,000? Another method of calculating a return that takes into account the time-value-of-money would calculate only a 4% rate-of-return. Doesn't sound so good now, does it? So, just like the term "payment," you need to know which return-on-investment method is being used to compute the return; not all are equal.

No or Low Money Down and ROI

Investing opportunities are available where little or no investment cash in required. If you generate a profit from an investment that required no cash (e.g. you are assuming a note with a property), it is mathematically impossible to compute a rate-of-return. Simply put, there is no percentage that can be calculated when the denominator of the formula is zero. Likewise, when a small amount of cash is invested with a disproportionate profit generated, the return-on- investment percentage can be so large that the meaningfulness of the calculation is substantially diminished.

> **Example 1**: Tom purchased a property worth $135,000 by paying the seller $1,000 and assuming the existing $100,000 mortgage. Tom sold the property six months later for the value. The profit of $35,000 ($135,000 - $100,000 loan payoff) divided by the small investment of $1,000 equals a return of 3,500%.

> **Example 2**: Tom buys another property worth $135,000 by paying the seller $1,000 and assuming the existing note of $133,500. The profit of $1,500 ($135,000 - $133,500 loan payoff) divided by the small investment of

$1,000 equals a return of 50%. A great percentage, but the $500 is not worth the risk and effort.

In situations where the return-on-investment calculation is not meaningful, substitute the cash flow or profit from the investment when evaluating this prong of the decision-making matrix.

Screening Tools

Another mistake we regularly see is investors assuming that all financial ratios are a return-on-investment calculation. Some financial ratios have very little to do with investment return but are merely screening devices to help sort through opportunities. Screening tools only measure a piece of the overall puzzle and should not be used in isolation for investment decision-making.

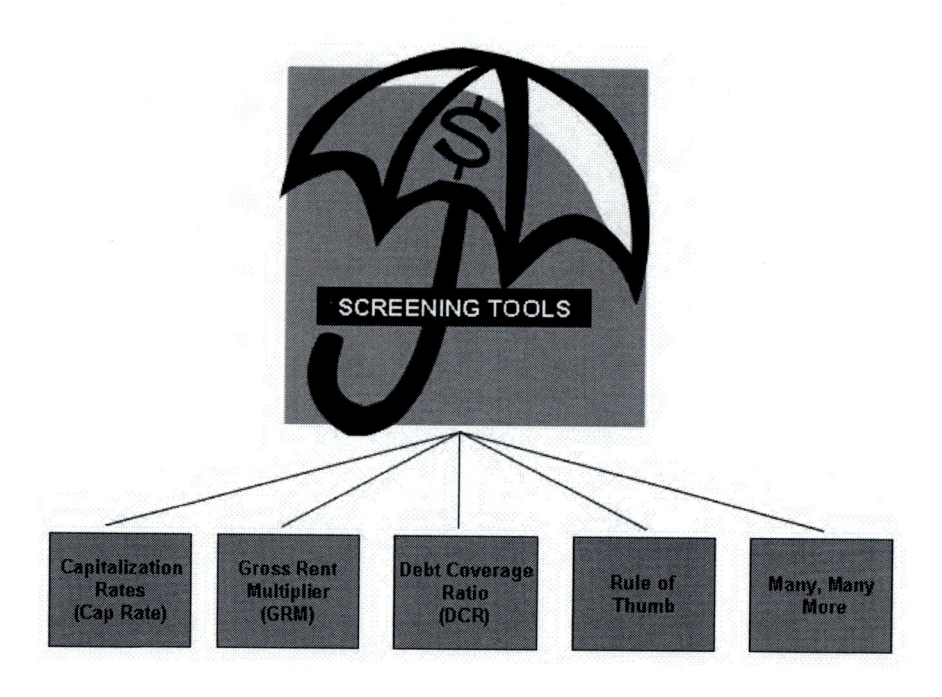

SCREENING TOOLS

- Capitalization Rates (Cap Rate)
- Gross Rent Multiplier (GRM)
- Debt Coverage Ratio (DCR)
- Rule of Thumb
- Many, Many More

Time and Effort

I frequently see investors make investment decisions based solely on a return-on-investment calculation. Many investors will calculate a return, say 25%, and then quickly decide to make a purchase. Remember, real estate investing can consume more of your time than most other investments. Therefore, make sure you are compensated for your **time and effort.**

> **Note:** Your time consumption will also vary drastically based on the type of real estate investment, e.g. multi-family, raw land, commercial or residential.

The incremental increase in rate-of-return must compensate you for your time, the risk, and the lost rate-of-return the cash would have generated from another investment. The premise is simple, when investing in a time-consuming investment, consider yourself in a partnership with your cash. Both you and your partner (cash) need to be adequately compensated.

I never knew I had a partner!

Valuing your time

How much is your time worth? The value of your time and effort, of course, is relative and subjective. A young single person will value his personal time quite differently than an older married man with four children. You will need to assign a value of your time based on a number of factors, but probably the easiest way to assign a value is to calculate opportunity cost.

Opportunity cost is essentially defined as the money or compensation you are giving up so that you can do something else. As an example, let's assume you have a job making $20 an hour. The rental property you want to purchase will require ten hours a week to manage. Spending ten hours a week at the new property will mean that you will not be able to work those same hours at your existing job. You would value that time at $200 per week ($20 x 10 hours) or about $1,000 a month. Thus, you need to make certain that the rental property will not only deliver a reasonable return on your cash, but also compensate you for your lost wages.

> **Note:** When evaluating opportunity cost, the above example may be too simplistic. Using an hourly calculation fails to consider that your time may be creating a business enterprise that will continue to pay dividends for many years to come. The calculation also fails to consider that you may lose your existing job because the employer may not be happy with the reduced hours.

Of course, the premise behind opportunity cost is that there is truly a cost. If you were not able to work those ten hours (e.g. you are working the maximum hours already) then you really may not have an opportunity cost. So, when calculating your opportunity cost, you need to be honest and not fool yourself.

Chapter 4

Leveraging

Real estate investors generally borrow money or leverage when they invest to maximize return and the number of properties they can own. For example, an investor who has $100,000 in cash could buy one property for $100,000 or leverage his money and buy five $100,000 properties by putting $20,000 down and borrowing $80,000 on each property.

Leveraging is a technique that, if used properly, can exponentially increase investment returns. However, leveraging only makes sense if the investment will yield a higher return than the interest rate charged for the loan. In other words, you generally only want to leverage if you can take the borrowed money and invest it in a manner that will generate at least enough money to pay for the loan.

For example, you would never take out a loan, say at 7%, to invest in a money market account returning only 3%. In that case, you would have a negative 4% return. The same principle applies to real estate investing.

Investors with plenty of cash frequently ask me whether they should borrow or use their own money. There are certain circumstances when borrowing does not make sense.

As I mentioned earlier, one of the purposes of leveraging is to increase the number of properties an investor can own; however, if your goal is to own only a few properties and you have the cash to purchase them, you may want to use your own money.

For example, let's assume Tom has $300,000 in cash in his Individual Retirement Account (IRA). Tom wants to diversify his retirement holdings by investing in three $100,000 properties. Using the Cash Flow Analyzer® software, Tom has determined that these properties will generate a 20% return-on-investment, have very little risk, and will not consume too much of his time. Since Tom is just forty years old, he has no need for his retirement money for at least twenty-five years.

Tom has the option of borrowing $210,000 from a bank at 9% to make the three purchases or using all $300,000 of his IRA cash. Which option should Tom select? To answer that question, we need to know what he anticipates the return will be on his remaining IRA money if he decides to borrow.

Assuming that he will only make a 4% money market rate-of-return on the remaining cash, his overall account value will actually be lower than if he used his own cash. On the other hand, if he were able to make more than 9% on the remaining cash, then he would be better off borrowing.

Should I Borrow?

Bank Loan Amount	$ 210,000
Loan Rate	9%
Interest Expense	18,900
Remaining IRA Cash	$ 210,000
Investment Opportunity	4%
Potential Earnings	8,400
Net Account Value Decrease	$ (10,500)

The above calculation shows that if Tom borrows and makes only a 4% return on the excess IRA cash, his account value will be $10,500 less than if he used his own money. Leveraging does **not** make sense in this case.

Chapter 5

Flipping vs. Speculating and Mortgage Fraud

For some, the term flipping has a negative connotation. In fact, some of our customers have suggested we should change the name of our product, the Flipper's Cash Flow Analyzer®, because of this. However, this negative connotation has generally resulted from misinformation. The two primary contributors to this negative connotation are speculators and perpetrators of mortgage fraud.

Speculators

Speculators are much like the stock traders during the recent stock market bubble. They simply cash in on the real estate frenzy by purchasing a property (or the right to purchase a property) and placing it back on the market without adding any value during the process except perhaps to their own bank accounts.

I have seen all sorts of crazy things like a contract on a beachfront condominium change hands four times before the actual complex was even built! This "trading" only resulted in artificially increasing the price for the ultimate buyer.

I do not recommend getting involved in speculating. Speculating is like a game of hot potato. If you are the one caught when the music stops, *you are out of the game!*

On the other hand, an investor who purchases an ugly or dilapidated property, fixes it up, and sells it in a few short months is actually improving not only that one property, but also the neighboring property values and the overall community-at-large.

27

Although some people feel that investors prey on the misfortunes of others, there is absolutely nothing illegal or immoral about buying a property from a distressed homeowner who needs to sell a property quickly for one reason or another (e.g. bankruptcy, job transfer, divorce, disability, or death). The value the investor is providing in this case is cash or liquidity to a homeowner when he needs it most.

Mortgage Fraud

Even though you may have heard or read that real estate flipping is illegal, it is not. There is nothing wrong with purchasing real estate and selling it regardless of how long you hold the property. The real issue is not really flipping, but mortgage fraud.

A particular type of mortgage fraud uses real estate flipping as a cover. Since real estate flipping has become so popular in recent years, people using this type of mortgage fraud have been able to blend in with the crowd of legitimate flippers. Of course, with the increase in mortgage fraud and its publicity, people associate fraud with flipping and thus assume that flipping is illegal.

Although there are many forms and variations on the theme, the actual mortgage fraud strategy is quite simple in concept. The fraudster purchases a property, say for $100,000, and colludes with an appraiser to issue a bogus appraisal report stating the property is worth $250,000. The appraisal may state that certain repairs or improvements were done when in fact they were not. The purchaser then takes this appraisal to a bank to refinance the property and pockets the refinance proceeds. The purchaser disappears and leaves the bank to foreclose on the property that is only worth $100,000.

This particular type of fraud has hit some neighborhoods and communities particularly hard and has hurt the real estate industry in general. On the other hand, true flipping has improved countless neighborhoods and infused much needed wealth into specific communities and the economy in general.

Flip Life Cycle

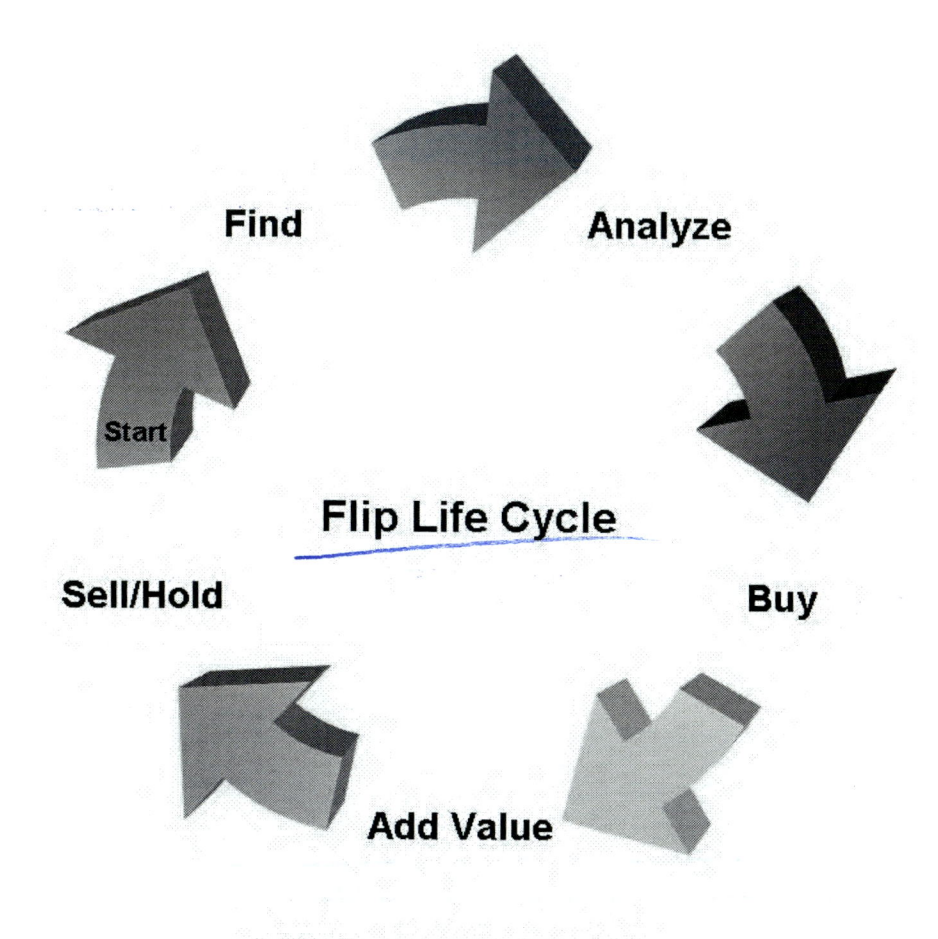

- Start
- Find
- Analyze
- Buy
- Add Value
- Sell/Hold

© 2007 LandlordSoftware.com LLC

Section II: Cash Flow Analysis

Chapter 6

Starting the Analysis Process

After identifying a property, the investment decision process actually begins with gathering the necessary information to do a **cash flow analysis**. Some information may be readily available from a real estate agent or from an investment package. Obtaining other information may take a little more effort, or you may have to make certain educated assumptions.

Many investors feel they need to have all the information before starting an analysis, but waiting can be costly. If the property is a good investment, rest assured, the opportunity will not last long.

Think of a cash flow analysis as a work in progress that you continually refine as you gather and verify information. Taking this approach will help you sort through properties much faster, resulting in fewer lost opportunities. If I do not have all the information, I estimate many of the variables so that I can quickly weed through the opportunities. From these, I select properties for further analysis and due diligence.

Due diligence is the process of researching, gathering, and verifying the information on a property so that a *final* purchase decision can be made. The due diligence process is also used to verify assumptions made and information provided by the seller. A cash flow analysis begins the due diligence period and is refined throughout the investment decision process. Only when a cash flow analysis meets your investment objectives will you make an offer. Your offer should contain contingencies allowing you to withdraw the offer if the information you relied on to make the offer is inaccurate or cannot be substantiated.

Some of the more common contingencies are as follows:

- Loan approval
- Property inspection
- Clean and clear title
- Review of seller's books and records
- Review of all rental applications and agreements

For income-producing properties, further due diligence is generally only performed after an offer has been accepted. Remember, tenants are usually occupying the property; therefore, this will be the first time you will be permitted to view the inside of the property. This is also the time that you will be permitted to verify the seller's financial information.

> **Note:** Usually when making an "as-is" offer, such as a bank foreclosure, due diligence must be completed prior to making the offer.

Chapter 7

Landlord's Cash Flow Analyzer® Software
What Information Do I Need?

Before any number crunching can begin, you first need to know what information is required. Therefore, this section is organized in the same manner as the software's Input Data Screen.

I. Rental Income and Expenses

How do I determine the income from a property?

Current lease documents or rental agreements are probably the best source for determining the amount you will be able to charge for rent; however, keep in mind that mismanaged properties may have rents well below the current market rate. If the property is being rented, ask to see the lease agreement or, at least, ask for the following information:

- What is (are) the current amount of rent(s) being charged?
- What have been the historical lease increases?
- When does (do) the lease(s) expire?
- How long has (have) the tenant(s) been leasing?
- What is the seller's opinion of tenant(s)?
- What are the lease terms? Renewable?
- Does (do) the tenant(s) intend to renew?

Obviously, a property that is currently not renting will not have a lease agreement for you to examine. In that case, you need to seek other sources such as real estate agents, landlords with rentals in the area, and property management companies. Rentalhouses.com is another great source for finding market rental rates in your area. Of course, you can list your properties with them as well.

How do I determine my vacancy rate?

As a landlord, you will periodically have vacancies due to turnover or renovation. The vacancy rate is an average that is expressed as a percentage of gross rents, e.g. 4%. Determining the actual vacancy rate is difficult because it is hard to predict how long your tenants will actually stay and how long it will take to replace them. Furthermore, if you have a lengthy tenant eviction, your vacancy rate can dramatically differ from what you predicted.

A projected vacancy rate should be expressed as the number of months you expect the property to be vacant in a given period of time. For example, a 4.1% vacancy rate is calculated by dividing 1 by 24. This means that on average, you expect the property to be vacant one month out of every two years. A 5.6% projected vacancy rate would mean one out of eighteen months, and an 8.33% projected vacancy rate would mean one out of twelve months.

If the property is currently being leased or rented, ask the seller for the historical vacancy rate to use in the cash flow analysis, assuming that the rate appears reasonable. If the information is not available, talk with other landlords in the area and estimate. You may wish to run several analyses using different rates to determine the impact.

Note: Mismanaged properties can have very high vacancy rates. This can represent an opportunity for the savvy investor.

For commercial properties or multi-unit apartments, apply the same concept to each unit or lease and then calculate a blended rate.

33

What expenses should I expect and how do I determine them?

Every property will have insurance expense, property taxes, repairs and maintenance, utility expense, and, usually, interest expense. If the property is rented, the seller should be able to provide a list of the historical expenses. If not, most of the expenses such as insurance and interest are easy to determine. The county's property tax office, insurance agents, and mortgage brokers can be helpful in providing this information.

Other expenses, such as repairs and maintenance, can be more difficult to estimate. Factors such as the age and condition of the property have a direct impact on how much you will have to spend over the years. Generally, older properties need more maintenance.

Tip: A thorough home inspection is a great tool for identifying future repairs.

Landlords sometimes fail to consider *who* will be doing the repairs and maintenance. If you plan on being your own handyman, make sure that you have considered this in the time and effort prong of the decision-making process.

If you will not be doing the repairs yourself, keep in mind that labor can be expensive and finding the right people takes time and patience. As an investor, you must keep expenses to a minimum, but you cannot afford to hire an incompetent and unreliable handyman who causes more damage to your property than he is attempting to repair.

Tip: Your tenants will view the handyman as a reflection of you, so consider your handyman's appearance and manners as well.

II. Property Costs and Characteristics

Cost

Of course, to do a cash flow analysis, you will need to know what you expect to pay for the property, or at least, the current listing price. The cost of the property is also used to determine the down payment (the check you will have to write) by subtracting the amount you plan to borrow from the cost.

> **Tip**: Keep in mind that the software will also solve for the exact offer price (i.e. your cost) that will meet your investment objectives.

Type

The cost, type of property (e.g., commercial, residential, mobile home), and the land value also determines the amount of tax depreciation, and thus tax benefit, the property will generate. Land values can be obtained from local tax records and vary between 20% and 30% of the actual cost of the property.

Fair Market Value (FMV)

An accurate cash flow analysis must reflect the future sale of the property. The proceeds from the projected sale are used to determine a *total* return-on-investment. The projected sales proceeds are a function of three items: current fair market value, future appreciation, and future selling expenses.

The cost and the fair market value (FMV) of the property are often different. A seller's financial position, bank foreclosure, or a probate property often result in an opportunity to purchase a property for less than its true market value.

The Cash Flow Analyzer® has a separate data entry field for the property's FMV. The software uses the FMV when applying the annual appreciation rate and when calculating the profit from the future sale.

Appreciation Rate

As discussed earlier, many factors affect not only the value of a property but also how a property appreciates. Residential property is generally valued or appraised based on what similar houses, or comparables, have sold for in the area. Therefore, the value of your neighbor's house usually has a direct impact on the value of your house and vice versa. The rate of appreciation on your property will be in tandem with the increase in value of comparables.

After taking into consideration the previously listed factors that affect the value of a property, make an educated guess and enter the rate into the software.

> **Tip**: You can use the Cash Flow Analyzer ® software to quickly change your assumptions and determine the effects.

You can either enter the appreciation rate as an average or specify a separate rate for each year.

> **Example 1**: A $100,000 residential property is located in an area that has consistently appreciated at an average annual rate of 3%. Entering 3% as the annual rate in the software results in a fair market value calculation of $109,273 by year four.

> **Example 2**: This same residential property is in a *hot* real estate market. For the past two years, properties have appreciated 10% per year and are expected to continue at that rate for the next two years. Thereafter, the market is

expected to cool to 3%. In this circumstance, you must specify the rate yearly to get an accurate projection. The fair market value, in this case, is projected to be $128,369 by year four.

Commercial properties are generally not valued based on comparables but rather on their cash flow and rate-of-return. Thus, the appreciation of a commercial property is based on a function of an annual increase in its cash flow.

Calculating the value of a commercial property can be a bit of a circular equation because what you will pay for a commercial property directly affects the cash flow and rate-of-return, and the cash flow and rate-of-return directly affects what you will pay. The dilemma is almost a chicken or the egg scenario.

In a cash flow analysis, the projected sales price of a commercial property is "assigned" by dividing the property's net operating income (NOI) by a factor. This factor is called a capitalization rate (cap rate). For a more detailed discussion of capitalization rate, refer to the Financial Ratios section of this book.

> **Note:** I use the word "assigned" in the above paragraph because, as I mentioned, a cap rate does not determine the actual value or the sales price of a property. However, due to the circular nature of the calculation, you should use a cap rate for your starting point.

> **Example 3:** A commercial property has a NOI of $100,000 and the cap rate for the area is 7%. The projected value of the property using a 7% cap rate is $1,428,571 ($100,000/7%). Thus, the change in value (either up or down) from one year to the next is a function of the change in net operating income.

Example 4: The same commercial property has a NOI of $110,000 in the next year. The projected value of the property using a 7% cap rate is $1,571,429. The result is a change in value of $142,858 or 10% (the same percentage change in the net operating income).

Selling Expenses

Projected sales proceeds are reduced by selling expenses. Generally, selling expenses include real estate commissions (e.g. 6%) and incentives given to the buyer to purchase the property (e.g. paying 3% toward the buyer's closing costs).

Future Improvements

A cash flow analysis should include future property repairs and improvements. A property inspection report is helpful in identifying these items. For example, if the inspection report states that the roof must be replaced in three years, the third year of the cash flow analysis will need to reflect this cash outlay. Failing to incorporate future improvements and repairs can significantly affect your return-on-investment and even result in overpaying for a property.

III. Financing

As discussed earlier, borrowing can increase investment return and the potential number of properties you can own. Loan types include interest-only, negative amortization, adjustable rates (ARM), balloons, and traditional amortization. The type of loan, interest rate, and term (loan period) directly affect cash flow and rate-of-return.

Except for possibly the down payment, a mortgage payment is probably the single largest cash flow expense that you will have when owning a property; therefore, loan payments must be included in the cash flow analysis.

Generally, loan payments are made monthly and consist of an interest portion and a principal portion (except interest-only and negative amortization loans). Each component has a different impact on your cash flow analysis. The interest expense is tax deductible (generating a tax benefit) while the principal payment is not; however, the principal payment increases wealth as discussed in the equity from loan payments section.

For every loan type, period, and rate, you will have a different loan payment. The Cash Flow Analyzer® software will calculate these payments for you.

Tip: You can use the Cash Flow Analyzer® software to help you select the best type of loan for your situation.

IV. Income Taxes

A cash flow analysis includes the effects of income tax expense or benefit during the rental period and taxes owed on the future sale. To compute income taxes, you first need to compute taxable income which differs from a cash flow calculation. For example, as mentioned above, the principal portion of a loan is not tax deductible, but the interest portion is; and taxable income is also reduced by tax depreciation and the amortization of loan points. Tax expense is then determined by multiplying the computed taxable income by your "marginal" individual income tax rate.

Marginal Rate vs. Effective Rate

The United States federal tax system is a progressive tax system. The more you make, the more you "disproportionately" owe. The higher your income, the higher your tax rate will be on *all* of your income.

Example 1: Tom, a single person making $25,000, is in the 15% tax bracket. If Tom were to earn $100,000, his tax rate would jump to 28%.

Marginal rate is defined as the tax rate at which the next dollar of income is taxed. In the above example, if Tom earned an additional $1,000 from a rental activity above his $100,000 salary, Tom would pay $280 more in tax ($1,000 x 28%).

The effective rate, on the other hand, is the *average* income tax rate. This rate is calculated after taking into consideration tax items such as itemized deductions and personal exemptions. The effective rate is the *total* tax that you owe in a given tax year divided by either your *total* taxable income or your gross income.

> **Example 2**: Tom earns $25,000 and is entitled to a $5,350 standard deduction and a $3,400 personal exemption deduction. Tom's taxable income is computed as $16,250 ($25,000 - $5,350 - $3,400). The income tax, per the tax tables in the appendix of this book, is computed to be $2,046. The effective rate is 12.6% based on the computed taxable income and 8% based on the gross income even though Tom's marginal rate is 15%.

The marginal rate, not the effective rate, is used in a cash flow analysis to determine the *marginal* tax increase or decrease resulting from the proposed investment.

Passive Losses

A rental activity, as defined by the Internal Revenue Service (IRS), is a "passive" activity. Of course, any landlord will tell you that rental activity is far from being passive.

The term "passive", as it relates to taxes, was introduced in 1986 when the IRS began cracking down on abusive real estate tax shelters. The result was a new and complicated tax regime that imposed potential limitations on receiving tax benefits from rental activities. Tax losses limited by these rules are called "suspended" losses and are carried forward until offset by passive income or until the property that generated the loss is sold. As with any rule, there are exceptions to the passive activity limitation. The "real estate professional" exception and the $25,000-per-year "active participation" allowance are two examples.

If you are expecting to receive significant tax benefits from a property investment, you **must** make sure you are not limited by the passive activity rules or you will have a surprise waiting for you at tax time. Please consult a tax advisor or other professional as appropriate.

Tip: You can quickly determine the effects of the passive activity rules by selecting "yes" or "no" to the passive activity question in the Cash Flow Analyzer® software. If the effect is substantial, a consultation with a tax advisor may be prudent.

Capital Gain Taxes

The two kinds of tax rates are "ordinary" and "capital gain." Ordinary tax rates, which are much higher than capital gain rates, are used to compute income taxes due on such things as wages, interest income, and rental income. Capital gain rates are only computed on long-term gain from investments such as stock or real estate. Long-term in defined as more than twelve months. Currently, the maximum capital gain rate is 15%.

Real estate is a capital asset for tax purposes unless the seller is classified as a "dealer." For example, a builder is generally considered a dealer. Homes sold by builders are subject to ordinary income tax rates, not the favorable capital gain tax rates.

Example: Tom and Bill each sell a property they held for more than one year and each has a $100,000 taxable gain. They are both in the 28% marginal income tax bracket. Since Tom is a builder, he owes $28,000 in income taxes. Bill, on the other hand, is an investor and only owes

$15,000 since his property qualifies for the favorable capital gains tax. The difference of $13,000 in taxes owed is substantial.

Tax Depreciation Benefit

As mentioned earlier, tax depreciation is a deduction from your rental income. Since rental income is subject to ordinary tax rates, the depreciation is creating a taxable benefit using the higher ordinary tax rates. However, the tax depreciation benefit is only temporary, because the depreciation taken has to be added back in the year a property is sold. Therefore, the longer you hold a property, the more the tax depreciation allowed, and the longer it will be before you have to pay Uncle Sam.

When you eventually sell a property, you will need to compute your taxable gain from the sale. The gain is the net sale proceeds less your original cost, plus all of the previously deducted depreciation.

> **Example 1:** Tom purchased a residential property for $100,000 five years ago, and the total depreciation deducted on his tax returns over the years is $18,000. Assuming Tom sells the property for his original cost, Tom pays tax on $18,000 ($100,000 − $100,000 + $18,000).

Even though Tom must pay tax on all of the depreciation taken, the time value of the tax savings can be substantial. Even more substantial is the income tax rate "play." Capital gain is taxed at the favorable (lower) capital gains tax rate which creates a permanent tax savings!

> **Example 2:** Continuing with the above example and assuming a 28% marginal tax rate, depreciation deduction

42

generated $5,040. When Tom sells his property and pays Uncle Sam back, he only has to pay $2,700 ($18,000 x 15%). He has generated a permanent tax savings of $2,340! The longer Tom holds the property, the more tax depreciation and the more permanent tax savings.

If Tom were to die and pass the property on to his heirs, none of the previous depreciation would reduce the cost, nor would tax ever be paid on the appreciation generated up to Tom's death. Certainly it isn't a reason to die, but you can "rest in peace" knowing your heirs benefited from your foresight.

Recapture Tax

In 1997, Congress created a recapture tax that eliminated some of the "permanent" tax depreciation benefit we just covered. The Cash Flow Analyzer® software calculates this amount automatically. Figure 1 is a sample tax analysis report from the Cash Flow Analyzer® software.

Taxable Income Analysis - Operations

	Year 1	Year 2	Year 3
Net Operating Income from Report	$ 7,046	$ 7,187	$ 7,330
Tax Depreciation	(2,953)	(3,082)	(3,082)
Points Amortization	-	-	-
Interest Expense - Mortgage #1	(5,600)	(6,051)	(5,985)
Operating Taxable Income (Loss)	$ (1,508)	$ (1,946)	$ (1,736)
Fed & State Tax Rate on Rental Income	33.00%	33.00%	33.00%
Tax (Expense) Benefit from Operations	$ 498	$ 642	$ 573
Subject to Suspended Loss Rules?	No	Help	

Taxable Income Analysis - Property Sale

	Year 1	Year 2	Year 3
Adjusted Projected Sales Price	$ 102,884	$ 106,485	$ 110,212
Original Cost of Property	(105,750)	(105,750)	(105,750)
Improvements Made	-	-	-
Amortization Points Paid	-	-	-
Gain or (Loss) on Property	(2,866)	735	4,462
Accumulated Depreciation/Amortization	2,953	6,035	9,117
Taxable Gain (Loss) on Property Sale	$ 88	$ 6,770	$ 13,579
Capital Gain & State Rate on Sale	20.00%	20.00%	20.00%
Income Tax (Expense) Benefit	(18)	(1,354)	(2,716)
Recapture Tax (if any)	(9)	(604)	(912)
Total Tax (Expense) Benefit from Sale	$ (26)	$ (1,958)	$ (3,628)

Figure 1

Section III: Financial Ratios & Terms

Chapter 8

Net Operating Income (NOI)

Net operating income (NOI) is a property's gross rental income reduced by all its expenses except for loan payments and taxes. NOI is calculated as follows:

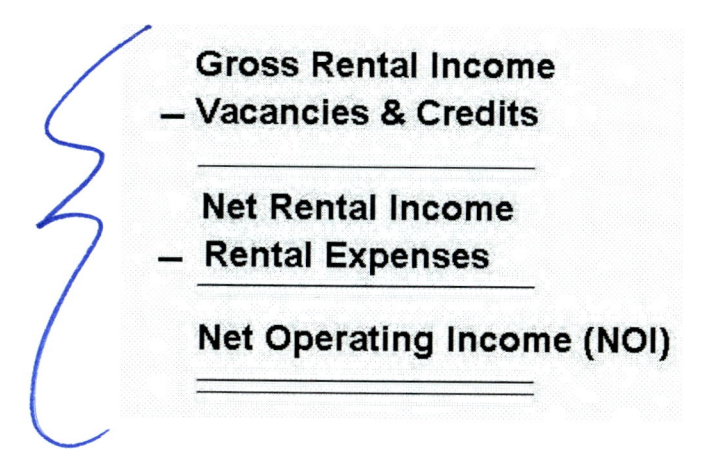

> **Gross Rental Income**
> **− Vacancies & Credits**
>
> **Net Rental Income**
> **− Rental Expenses**
>
> **Net Operating Income (NOI)**

NOI calculates the profitability of a particular property and is a significant component of a cash flow analysis. The NOI is also used as a screening tool for comparing properties. The NOI calculation does not include loan payments or income taxes because these two items can dramatically vary depending on the tax entity owning the property or debt structure.

Example 1: All things being equal, a property owned by a tax-exempt Individual Retirement Account (IRA) would

45

have a higher NOI than if it were owned by an individual if income taxes were a part of the NOI calculation.

Example 2: All things being equal, a property that had no debt would have a higher NOI than if the property were leveraged if loan payments were a part of the NOI calculation.

Using the NOI to screen properties is very useful, but you would never make an investment decision based on a NOI calculation. The NOI is only a small piece of the decision-making process.

Chapter 9

Present Value (PV) and Net Present Value (NPV)

A dollar that you will receive in the future may not have the same value as the dollar you have in your hand. If that is the case, then what is the value of that future dollar?

Present Value (PV) is a mathematical formula used to determine that value. Essentially, PV applies a discount or rate to reduce the face value of that future dollar (or a stream of future dollars) in an attempt to "translate" the future dollars into "present" day dollars.

Present Value (PV) Formula	Net Present Value (PV) Formula
$PV = C \cdot \dfrac{1 - \dfrac{1}{(1+i)^n}}{i}$	$NPV = \sum\limits_{t=1}^{T} \dfrac{C_t}{(1+r)^t} - C_o$
C = Investment, i = Rate, n = Years	C = Investment, r = Rate, t = Years

By way of example, let's assume that Tom has $10,000 in his savings account. Bill, on the other hand, won a small lottery and will receive $10,000 in five years. Do Tom and Bill have assets that are equal in value?

Table 1 illustrates that Tom makes 4% from his savings account, he will have $12,667 in five years, which is $2,667 more than what Bill will have when he receives his $10,000 payout. Therefore, Tom's asset is more valuable than Bill's based on a 4% discount rate.

	Value
End of Year 1	$10,400
End of Year 2	$10,816
End of Year 3	$11,249
End of Year 4	$11,699
End of Year 5	$12,167

Table 1

Since we know the "future value" of Tom's $10,000 investment to be $12,167, let's reverse it and solve for the "present value" of Bill's lottery ticket.

Using 4% in the PV formula above, the value of Bill's lottery ticket is determined to be $8,219. This is shown in Table 2. Based on a discount rate of 4%, Tom has an asset worth $10,000 and Bill has one worth $8,219.

	Value
End of Year 1	$ 8,548
End of Year 2	$ 8,890
End of Year 3	$ 9,245
End of Year 4	$ 9,615
End of Year 5	$ 10,000

Table 2

Note: Since PV uses a discount *rate*, the value of Bill's lottery ticket can change dramatically based on the rate used in the formula. A zero rate values the lottery ticket at $10,000 while a 30% rate values it at just $2,693.

Net Present Value (NPV) and **Present Value (PV)** are interconnected. NPV is the calculated PV less an initial investment. As an example, let's assume Tom plans to purchase a rental property for $100,000 with no debt. Table 3 shows Tom's estimated annual cash flow stream:

Investment In Property	(100,000)
Year 1 Cash Flow	5,500
Year 2 Cash Flow	3,500
Year 3 Cash Flow	(1,000)
Year 4 Cash Flow	3,500
Year 5 Cash Flow	3,500
Year 6 Cash Flow and Sale	222,500

Table 3

Using a 10% rate as our required rate-of-return, the present value of these future dollars is $137,300 as shown in Table 4. The net present value is $37,300, which is the present value of $137,300 less Tom's initial investment of $100,000.

Investment In Property	(100,000)		
Year 1 Cash Flow	5,500	$5,500 / 1.10 \wedge 1 =$	5,000
Year 2 Cash Flow	3,500	$3,500 / 1.10 \wedge 2 =$	2,893
Year 3 Cash Flow	(1,000)	$-1,000 / 1.10 \wedge 3 =$	(751)
Year 4 Cash Flow	3,500	$3,500 / 1.10 \wedge 4 =$	2,391
Year 5 Cash Flow	3,500	$3,500 / 1.10 \wedge 5 =$	2,173
Year 6 Cash Flow	222,500	$222,500 / 1.10 \wedge 6 =$	125,595
		Present Value (PV)	**$137,300**

Table 4

A "zero" net present value means that the investment is returning the exact rate that was entered into PV calculation. A net present value that is greater than zero means the investment is returning more than the rate entered. In the above example, the entered rate of 10% generated a NPV of $37,300. Therefore, the above investment is generating a return more than 10%.

Net Present Value (NPV) Matrix

If...	It means...
NPV > 0	The investment is generating **more** than your required rate-of-return.
NPV < 0	The investment is generating **less** than your required rate-of-return.
NPV = 0	The investment is generating **exactly** your required rate-of-return.

Note: Your "required" rate-of-return is the rate-of-return you are personally seeking to obtain.

Chapter 10

Internal Rate of Return (IRR)

n = number of cash flows
CF_j = cash flow at period j.
IRR = Internal Rate of Return

$$0 = \sum_{j=1}^{k} CF_j \cdot \left[\frac{1-(1+IRR)^{-n_j}}{IRR} \right] \cdot \left[(1+IRR)^{-\sum_{q<j} n_q} \right] + CF_0$$

While the present value (PV) and net present value (NPV) focus on calculating a "dollar" value of a cash flow stream based on a required rate-of-return, the **internal rate-of-return (IRR)** takes the same cash flow stream but solves for the actual "rate" or percentage that will calculate a zero net present value (NPV). Remember, a zero NPV means we are meeting our exact required rate-of-return.

In the net present value (NPV) calculation used in Chapter 9, we entered 10% as our required rate-of-return and determined that a NPV as $37,300. Based on the Net Present Value Matrix, we are generating more than a 10% return, but how much more we cannot determine using PV alone. The IRR is used to calculate the exact rate-of-return.

As you can see from the formula written above, calculating the IRR is complicated. However, using a financial calculator or Microsoft Excel ® will calculate an IRR of 16.33%.

> Note: If we had used 16.33% initially, rather than 10%, as our required rate-of-return for calculating the net present value of Tom's investment, the NPV would be zero. Using the Net Present Value Matrix, a zero NPV means we are generating our exact required rate-of-return or 16.33%.

51

Chapter 11

Modified Internal Rate of Return (MIRR)

The **modified internal rate-of-return (MIRR)** is the IRR calculation with modifications to correct an inherent fallacy. The IRR formula assumes that the annual cash flow is reinvested at the same rate as the ultimately calculated IRR. As an example, taking the previous cash flow stream, the IRR calculation assumes that the cash flow in the fourth year ($3,500) will be reinvested at 16.33%.

This fallacy in this assumption is that Tom will not realistically generate a 16.33% return on the $3,500 of cash flow because the cash will probably be deposited in a savings account earning something less like 4%. As a result, when you have a property that generates significant cash flow, the calculated IRR will overstate the likely financial return of the property.

The modified internal rate-of-return (MIRR) allows for an adjustment for this fallacy. The MIRR calculation allows you to enter a different rate-of-return, called the ***reinvestment rate,*** for the property's annual *positive* cash flow, and another rate, called the ***finance rate,*** for the property's *negative* cash flow. You may wish to assign a different rate to the negative cash flow if you borrow money to fund the outflow; however, it is perfectly acceptable for the ***reinvestment rate*** and ***finance rate*** to be the same.

> **Note:** Using the MIRR, a 4% reinvestment rate and finance rate yields a return of 15.6%.

Chapter 12

Debt Coverage Ratio (DCR)

Debt coverage ratio (DCR), also known as the **debt service coverage ratio (DSCR)**, measures the ability to pay the property's loan payments. Obviously, lenders are concerned about being repaid, so they use this ratio to determine if enough cash will be generated to pay not only the rental expenses, but also the loan payments.

The DCR is calculated by dividing the property's annual net operating income (NOI) by the property's annual debt service. Annual debt service is the annual total of all mortgage payments (i.e. the principal and accrued interest but not escrow payments).

$$\text{Debt Coverage Ratio} = \frac{\text{Net Operating Income}}{\text{Annual Debt Payments}}$$

> **Example**: Assume a net operating income of $20,000 and debt payments of $15,000. The DCR is 1.33 ($20,000 ÷ $15,000 = 1.33).

A debt coverage ratio of less than one (e.g. .75) indicates that there is not enough cash flow to pay the property's rental expenses and as well as the mortgage payments. Generally, a lender will not lend money to purchase a property that does not generate adequate cash. In the above example, the DCR of 1.33 means that the property will generate 1.33 times, or 33%, more cash than is needed to pay the loan ($5,000 / $15,000).

> **Tip**: Lenders generally look for a DCR of about 1.2, i.e. a property that generates 20% more in annual cash than the loan payments.

Chapter 13

Cash-on-Cash Return

Cash-on-cash return is probably the most important ratio when evaluating the long-term performance of a property. Cash-on-cash return calculates the annual "cash dividend" yield of an investment. The yield is the ratio of the annual net cash generated divided by the net cash required to make the investment. In real estate, cash-on-cash return is the property's annual "net" cash flow divided by the net investment, expressed as a percentage. The net investment in the property is the cost of the property minus the amount borrowed (i.e. the down payment).

$$\text{Cash-on-Cash Return} = \frac{\text{Net Annual Cash Flow}}{\text{Net Investment in Property}}$$

> **Example**: If the net cash flow from a property is $10,000, and the initial cash invested in the property is $100,000, the cash-on-cash return is calculated to be 10% ($10,000 ÷ $100,000).

The cash-on-cash return calculation does have certain limitations since it merely provides an annual snapshot of the investment. "Net" cash flow does not include appreciation (because appreciation is not recognized until the year of sale), the reduction of debt from loan payments, the accumulation of any cash generated from previous years, or adjust for the time-value-of-money.

The longer the investment period, the more important the annual cash flow is compared to the property's appreciation and debt reduction. Therefore, the longer you plan to hold a property, the more significant cash-on-cash return becomes in your decision-making process. The longer the investment time-period, the longer it is before appreciation and equity build-up are actually realized. As with any investment, uncertainty and risk can increase with time.

Chapter 14

Cash-on-Cash Return with Equity Build-Up

$$\text{CASH-on-CASH RETURN with EQUITY BUILD-UP} = \frac{\text{This Year's Net Cash Flow + Net Increase in Appreciation + Principal Reduction in Debt.}}{\text{Initial Investment in Property + Prior Year's Net Cash Generated + Net Appreciation + Debt Reduction}}$$

The **cash-on-cash return with equity build-up** adjusts the traditional cash-on-cash return to compensate for a few of the limitations listed in Chapter 13. The modified version of this ratio takes into consideration the annual change of the following:

- Appreciation
- Debt reduction from the loan payments
- The projected sales expenses
- Projected income taxes from the sale

Adding the above items together is the property's change in "net" equity. The modified ratio essentially treats this change as cash received even though it is not yet realized. The result is an "accrued" return-on-investment.

The initial investment in the property, the denominator, is also adjusted by all prior generated cash flow, appreciation, and debt reduction and reduced by the projected sales expense and projected income taxes from the sale. However, even with these adjustments, the ratio still only provides an annual snapshot and does not consider the time-value-of-money.

Use the change in "net" equity in the numerator when calculating this ratio. In general, equity is calculated by taking the property's fair market value and subtracting the outstanding loan balance. The annual change in equity is simply the increase or decrease in equity from one year to the next; "Net" equity is the equity reduced for future selling expenses and projected income taxes from the sale.

Using only the change in equity without adjusting for sales expenses and income taxes will inflate the calculated result. For example, if you own an investment property with an appraised value of $250,000 with an outstanding loan of $100,000, you will have $150,000 of equity. However, when you sell the property, you will only net $85,000 if you incur $65,000 of real estate commissions and income taxes. Your purchase decision may have been different using $85,000 as the projected sales proceeds rather than $150,000.

Chapter 15

Capitalization Rate (Cap Rate)

The **capitalization rate** is a ratio that places (or assigns) a value on a property based on the net operating income (NOI) generated. The cap rate is a screening tool that allows for a comparison of properties with different fair market values (FMV) and assigns a "starting" value for the cash flow analysis. The cap rate is computed by taking the NOI and dividing it by the property's FMV or cost. The higher the cap rate, the better the property is said to be performing. Essentially, the higher the cap rate, the more NOI the property is generating per dollar of FMV or cost.

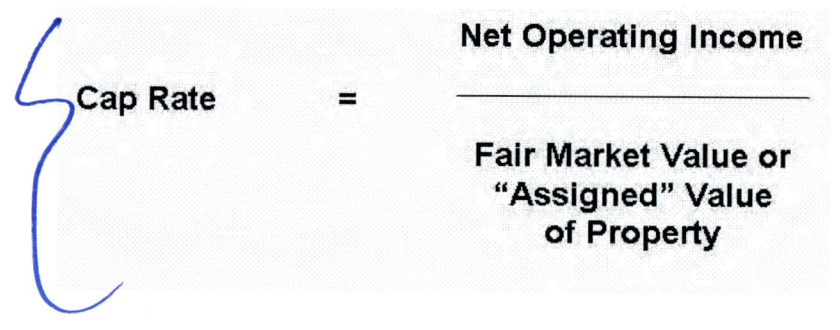

$$\text{Cap Rate} = \frac{\text{Net Operating Income}}{\text{Fair Market Value or ``Assigned'' Value of Property}}$$

A cap rate does not define or assign the *actual* value of the property. The cap rate's computed or assigned value is merely a starting point in the overall valuation process. As such, a cap rate is not a computation of investment return, but rather only a tool used in the calculation of an investment return. Cap rates do not consider significant items like initial investment, net cash flow, cost of debt, or income taxes.

$$\text{Fair Market Value or "Assigned" Value of Property} = \frac{\text{Net Operating Income}}{\text{Capitalization Rate}}$$

Example 1: A property generates $10,000 of annual net operating income. Using a sample 4% cap rate, the value is calculated as $250,000 ($10,000 ÷ .04).

Example 2: Two properties are available for purchase. The first property has a projected **NOI** of $20,000 and an asking price of $500,000. The second property has a **NOI** of only $10,000 with an asking price of $110,000. Which one would the cap rate suggest is a better investment? The second property is assumed to be a better investment since the cap rate is 9% ($10,000 ÷ $110,000) versus 4% ($20,000 ÷ $500,000).

As with anything, the calculated cap rate is only as good as the numbers used in the calculation. A perfect example involves deferred maintenance. If an owner ignores property maintenance, the property's NOI will be higher than it should be. If you make a purchase based on an incorrect NOI, not only will you overpay for the property, but you will also inherit all of the deferred maintenance.

Chapter 16

Loan-to-Value Ratio (LVR)

The **Loan-to-value ratio** is the amount of a secured loan or mortgage divided by the fair market value of the property. The LVR helps you quickly determine how leveraged your property is based on the fair market value of the property versus your cost. You can also use the LVR to determine the amount of your equity. If you have more than one loan secured against your property, add together the outstanding balance of each loan to calculate the LVR.

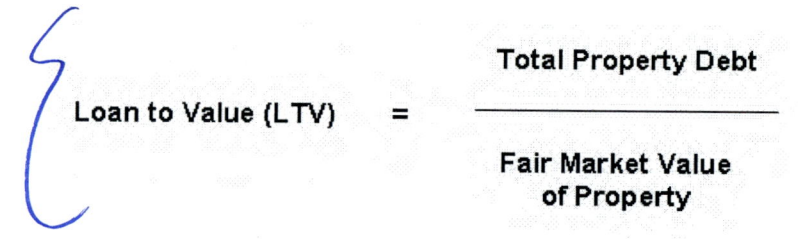

$$\text{Loan to Value (LTV)} = \frac{\text{Total Property Debt}}{\text{Fair Market Value of Property}}$$

Example: A home is worth $100,000 and has a mortgage balance of $50,000. The loan-to-value ratio is 50%. However, if you also have a second outstanding loan of $25,000, the loan-to-value ratio changes to 75% (($50,000 + $25,000) divided by $100,000).

Chapter 17

Gross Rent Multiplier (GRM)

The **gross rent multiplier (GRM)** is another way to screen and compare properties. Used mostly in the apartment industry, the GRM is much like the capitalization rate except gross rental income rather than net operating income (NOI) is used. The GRM is calculated by dividing the fair market value of the property by the gross rental income.

The GRM is also used to determine the number of years the property will take to pay for itself in gross rents received. The lower the GRM, the better the investment is assumed to be.

$$\text{Gross Rent Multiplier (GRM)} = \frac{\text{Fair Market Value of Property}}{\text{Annual Gross Rental Income}}$$

Example: If the sales price for a property is $200,000, and the annual gross rental income for a property is $30,000, the GRM is equal to 6.67 ($200,000 ÷ $30,000).

Section IV: Sample Analyses

Chapter 18

Sample Analysis #1 – Residential Rental Property

Sample Analysis #1 uses the following assumptions to generate the cash flow analysis report found on the following page:

Estimated Holding Period	3 years
Asking Price:	$ 105,000
Appreciation Rate	3.5%
Closing Costs	750
Future Commission on Sale	6%
Monthly Rent:	1,050
Annual Increase in Rents:	2%
Expected Vacancy:	1 month out of 24, or 4.2%
Property Taxes	2,425
Insurance	1,100

Maintenance		1,500
Annual Increase in Expenses:		2%
Borrowing 80% for 30 years at:		7.25%
Marginal Tax Rates:	Federal:	28.00%
	Capital Gains:	15.00%
	State Rate:	5.00%
No passive-loss rule limitation		

Note: The report is significantly modified with certain ratios, calculations, and other items removed for illustration purposes. Although you would normally hold a rental property for longer than three years, I have shortened the report for simplicity.

3-Year Cash Flow Analysis

Rental Activity Analysis		Year 1	Year 2	Year 3
Gross Rental Income	$	12,600	$ 12,852	$ 13,109
Vacancy & Credits		(529)	(540)	(551)
Operating Expenses		(5,025)	(5,126)	(5,228)
Net Operating Income (NOI)	$	7,046	$ 7,187	$ 7,330
Total Mortgage Payments		(6,348)	(6,925)	(6,925)
Capital Improvements		-	-	-
Operating Income Taxes: Benefit / (Expense)		498	642	573
Net CASH FLOW from Rent Activity	$	1,195	$ 903	$ 978

Item A → (6,925)
Item B → 978

Property Sale Analysis				
Projected Sale Price	$	109,451	$ 113,282	$ 117,247
Selling Expenses		(6,567)	(6,797)	(7,035)
Adjusted Projected Sales Price		102,884	106,485	110,212
Mortgage Balance Payoff		(83,852)	(82,977)	(82,036)
Income Taxes From Sale: Benefit / (Expense)		(26)	(1,958)	(3,628)
Net CASH FLOW from Property Sale	$	19,006	$ 21,551	$ 24,548

Item C → 24,548

Financial Ratios			
Debt Coverage Ratio (DCR)	1.11	1.04	1.06
Loan to Value Ratio (LVR)	76.6%	73.2%	70.0%

Cash on Cash Return with Equity BuildUp	-4.49%	17.07%	16.81%
Cash on Cash Return before Taxes	3.30%	1.24%	1.91%
Cash on Cash Return after Taxes	5.65%	4.27%	4.62%
Cumulative Internal Rate of Return (IRR)	-4.49%	5.90%	9.75%
Modified Internal Rate of Return (MIRR)	-4.49%	5.85%	9.49%
MIRR Reinvestment Rate:	4.00%		
MIRR Finance Rate:	7.25%		

Item D → 16.81%
Item E → 9.75%

The property is projected to generate approximately $1,000 a year in net positive cash flow as indicated by <u>item</u> **B**. Based on the net investment of $21,150 ($105,750 less the $84,600 loan), the **cash-on-cash return** is approximately 4.7% after taxes. However, as indicated by <u>item</u> **A,** almost 60% of the cash flow generated is from income tax benefits.

As indicated by <u>item</u> **C**, the property has a projected cash flow from sale in Year 3 of $24,548. Subtracting the initial investment of $21,150 ($105,750 less the $84,600 loan), the "net" equity increase is only $3,398. While the **cash-on-cash return with equity build-up return** of 16.81% (<u>Item</u> **D**) appears to be acceptable, the result is quite misleading. The reason is that the ratio only takes into consideration the "change" in net equity and ignores previous effects. The first year's cash-on-cash return with equity build-up return took into account the full 6% sales expense and generated a loss of 4.49%. Year 3 only takes into account the "change" that is small from Year 2 to Year 3. As indicated in Chapter 14, this ratio is only a snapshot of the year and ignores the cumulative cash generated or lost and does not consider the time-value-of-money.

> **Note:** Cash-on-cash return with equity build-up ratio for Year 3 was calculated by adding the net cash flow of $978, as indicated by <u>item</u> **B,** to the change in "net" equity from Year 2 to Year 3 of $2,997 ($24,548 minus $21,551, per <u>item</u> **C**) for a total of $3,975. That number is divided by our adjusted investment in the property, $23,649 ($21,150 initial investment plus $2,098 net cash flow generated for the previous two years plus $401 of equity build-up from the previous years) for a 16.81% return as indicated by <u>item</u> **D**.

Since this example only looks at the first three years of the ownership, any decision to purchase should be made using the internal-rate-of-return (IRR). The IRR accounts for all of the net cash flow, the net sales proceeds, and time-value-of-money. As such, the IRR will give a more realistic rate-of-return.

The IRR of 9.75% in Year 3 (<u>item</u> **E**) is the "return" component of the three-pronged decision-making matrix. Of course, the other two components to be evaluated are "risk" and "time and effort."

> **Note:** A shorter holding period generally results in a low return because the property's value has less time to grow to overcome the impact of a sales commission.

65

Goal Seek Example

The Cash Flow Analyzer® also solves backwards to determine the maximum purchase price you could pay to achieve a desired rate-of-return. Let's assume that you want a 15% internal rate-of-return by Year 3. Select the Goal Seek tab of the Cash Flow Analyzer and enter 15% where indicated. Clicking "Seek Answer" will result in the calculated amount of $84,690. This is the maximum you can pay for the property to generate a 15% IRR.

Note: This is an excellent way to quickly determine your offer price for a property based on your desired rate-of-return. You can also solve backwards for the necessary sales price, rental income or cash-on-cash return.

Goal Seeking & Sensitivity Analysis

Current Input

Initial Gross Monthly Rent	1,050	Original Purchase Price: 105,750
Rental Appreciation Rate	2.00%	Original Fair Market Value: 105,750
		Property Appreciation Rate: 3.50%

Solve for Property Purchase Price by Changing IRR

To achieve an **IRR** of 15.00% by Year 3 with a Property Appreciation rate of 3.50%

The Purchase Price must be $ 84,690 Compared to Existing Input of $ 105,000 and IRR of 9.75%

Solve for Property Purchase Price by Changing MIRR

To achieve an **MIRR** of 15.00% by Year 3 with a Property Appreciation rate of 3.50%

The Purchase Price must be $ 81,345 Compared to Existing Input of $ 105,000 and MIRR of 9.49%

Chapter 19

Sample Analysis #2 – Residential Rental Property, continued

Let's take the same property but evaluate years ten through twelve.

Years 10, 11, 12 -Year Cash Flow Analysis
Version 1

Rental Activity Analysis

	Year 10	Year 11	Year 12
Gross Rental Income	$ 15,058	$ 15,359	$ 15,667
Vacancy & Credits	(632)	(645)	(658)
Operating Expenses	(6,005)	(6,125)	(6,248)
Net Operating Income (NOI)	$ 8,420	$ 8,589	$ 8,761
Total Mortgage Payments	(6,925)	(6,925)	(6,925)
Capital Improvements	-	-	-
Operating Income Taxes: Benefit / (Expense)	9	(85)	(183)
Net CASH FLOW from Rent Activity	$ 1,504	$ 1,578	$ 1,652

A ←
B ←

Property Sale Analysis

	Year 10	Year 11	Year 12
Projected Sale Price	$ 149,171	$ 154,392	$ 159,796
Selling Expenses	(8,950)	(9,264)	(9,588)
Adjusted Projected Sales Price	140,221	145,128	150,208
Mortgage Balance Payoff	(73,154)	(71,477)	(69,674)
Income Taxes From Sale: Benefit / (Expense)	(16,101)	(18,007)	(19,948)
Net CASH FLOW from Property Sale	$ 50,966	$ 55,644	$ 60,586

Financial Ratios

	Year 10	Year 11	Year 12
Debt Coverage Ratio (DCR)	1.22	1.24	1.26
Loan to Value Ratio (LVR)	49.0%	46.3%	43.6%
Cash on Cash Return with Equity BuildUp	10.40%	9.93%	9.52%
Cash on Cash Return before Taxes	7.07%	7.86%	8.68%
Cash on Cash Return after Taxes	7.11%	7.46%	7.81%
Cumulative Internal Rate of Return (IRR)	13.07%	13.01%	12.93%
Modified Internal Rate of Return (MIRR)	11.92%	11.78%	11.64%

C ←
D ←

As indicated by item **A**, the large tax benefit from earlier years is now beginning to turn into an expense. Our taxable income is

67

increasing at a faster pace than our expenses, and the annual interest expense is less from normal loan amortization.

The net cash flow (item B) is about 50% higher than in the early years, so our **cash-on-cash** return has jumped to a healthier 7.81% (item C). The internal-rate-of-return has increased as well to about 13% (as indicated in item D). This investment is becoming more attractive.

The major problem with the example is that we have assumed no additional capital expenditures. A mere $5,000 improvement in Year 10 (item A) reduces the internal-rate-of-return by almost 1% (item B) as indicated in version 2.

Years 10, 11, 12 -Year Cash Flow Analysis
Version 2

Rental Activity Analysis

	Year 10	Year 11	Year 12
Gross Rental Income	$ 15,058	$ 15,359	$ 15,667
Vacancy & Credits	(632)	(645)	(658)
Operating Expenses	(6,005)	(6,125)	(6,248)
Net Operating Income (NOI)	$ 8,420	$ 8,589	$ 8,761
Total Mortgage Payments	(6,925)	(6,925)	(6,925)
Capital Improvements	(5,000)	-	-
Operating Income Taxes: Benefit / (Expense)	66	(25)	(123)
Net CASH FLOW from Rent Activity	$ (3,439)	$ 1,638	$ 1,712

(5,000 is circled with an arrow labeled A)

Property Sale Analysis

	Year 10	Year 11	Year 12
Projected Sale Price	$ 149,171	$ 154,392	$ 159,796
Selling Expenses	(8,950)	(9,264)	(9,588)
Adjusted Projected Sales Price	140,221	145,128	150,208
Mortgage Balance Payoff	(73,154)	(71,477)	(69,674)
Income Taxes From Sale: Benefit / (Expense)	(15,153)	(17,114)	(19,109)
Net CASH FLOW from Property Sale	$ 51,914	$ 56,537	$ 61,424

Financial Ratios

	Year 10	Year 11	Year 12
Debt Coverage Ratio (DCR)	1.22	1.24	1.26
Loan to Value Ratio (LVR)	49.0%	46.3%	43.6%
Cash on Cash Return with Equity BuildUp	3.40%	10.61%	10.11%
Cash on Cash Return before Taxes	-16.57%	7.86%	8.68%
Cash on Cash Return after Taxes	-16.26%	7.75%	8.09%
Cumulative Internal Rate of Return (IRR)	**12.31%**	**12.29%**	**12.24%**
Modified Internal Rate of Return (MIRR)	**11.21%**	**10.91%**	**10.84%**

(12.24% is circled with an arrow labeled B)

Chapter 20

Sample Analysis #3 – Distressed Sale

This is an example of an investment for the investor who seeks short-term substantial appreciation by purchasing a property from a distressed homeowner and paying well below market value. The investor fully understands that the property will generate a negative annual cash flow, but expects (i.e. hopes and prays) the property will appreciate enough to cover the expenses and generate a sizable profit.

When an investor uses this strategy, the investor usually seeks an interest-only or a negative amortization loan to reduce his negative annual cash flow. Generally, these types of loans are quite dangerous but can be appropriate if the investor is experienced, knowledgeable, and liquid. In addition, the investment is generally held for a short period of time. The loans are dangerous because a market downturn can eliminate the premise of the investment strategy, leaving a devalued home and high debt in its wake. As discussed in Chapter 2, money and wealth are made in real estate from three components: rental cash flow, equity build-up from loan amortization, and appreciation. This strategy takes two of the three components off the table leaving only one: appreciation.

Here are the assumptions for this example:

Estimated Holding Period		3 years
Asking Price:	$	**550,000**
Initial improvements		12,000
Closing Costs		1,750
Current FMV - Distressed Sale	$	**650,000**
Appreciation Rate		**8.0%**
Future Commission on Sale		6.0%
Monthly Rent:		1,450
Annual Increase in Rents:		2.0%
Expected Vacancy:		0%
Property Taxes		4,425
Insurance		1,750
Maintenance		800
Homeowners Association		400
Annual Increase in Expenses:		2%
Borrowing 80% for 30 years at:		8.00%
		Interest-Only
Marginal Tax Rates:	Federal:	28.00%
	Capital Gains:	15.00%
	State Rate:	5.00%
Limited by the passive-loss rules		

3-Year Cash Flow Analysis

Rental Activity Analysis

	Year 1	Year 2	Year 3
Gross Rental Income	$ 17,400	$ 17,748	$ 18,103
Vacancy & Credits	-	-	-
Operating Expenses	(7,375)	(7,523)	(7,673)
Net Operating Income (NOI)	$ 10,025	$ 10,226	$ 10,430
Total Mortgage Payments	(33,073)	(36,080)	(36,080)
Operating Income Taxes: Benefit / (Expense)	-	-	-	← A
Net CASH FLOW from Rent Activity	$ (23,048)	$ (25,855)	$ (25,650)	← B

Property Sale Analysis

	Year 1	Year 2	Year 3
Projected Sale Price	$ 702,000	$ 758,160	$ 818,813
Selling Expenses	(42,120)	(45,490)	(49,129)
Adjusted Projected Sales Price	659,880	712,670	769,684
Mortgage Balance Payoff	(451,000)	(451,000)	(451,000)
Tax Benefit - Suspended Losses (if any)	12,824	26,801	40,711	← C
Income Taxes From Sale: Benefit / (Expense)	(23,970)	(39,478)	(55,831)
Net CASH FLOW from Property Sale	$ 197,734	$ 248,994	$ 303,564

Cash Position

	Year 1	Year 2	Year 3
Net Cash Generated This Year	$ (23,048)	$ (25,855)	$ (25,650)
Net Cumulative Cash Generated Previous Years	n/a	(23,048)	(48,903)
Net Cash Generated - Property Sale	197,734	248,994	303,564
Cash Inflow (Outflow) From Refinancing	-	-	-
Initial Investment	(112,750)	(112,750)	(112,750)
Total Net CUMULATIVE CASH Generated	$ 61,936	$ 87,341	$ 116,261	← D

Financial Ratios

	Year 1	Year 2	Year 3
Debt Coverage Ratio (DCR)	0.30	0.28	0.29
Loan to Value Ratio (LVR)	64.2%	59.5%	55.1%
Cash on Cash Return with Equity BuildUp	54.93%	14.54%	14.45%
Cash on Cash Return before Taxes	-20.44%	-22.93%	-22.75%
Cash on Cash Return after Taxes	-20.44%	-22.93%	-22.75%
Cumulative Internal Rate of Return (IRR)	54.93%	30.83%	23.24%	← E
Modified Internal Rate of Return (MIRR)	54.93%	28.93%	21.04%

As reflected by line **B**, the property will generate approximately $74,500 of negative cash flow over the first three years. However, since the property has built-in equity from the bargain purchase, the cash generated after only Year 1 would be $61,936 if sold as indicated by line **D**. The result is a 55% internal-rate-of-return as indicated by line **E**, since the "bargain-purchase pop" is recognized the first year. In Year 3, the internal-rate-of-return drops by more than half because "bargain-purchase pop" is spread out over a three-year period instead of just one.

Many investors jump to the conclusion that they should sell a property when the internal-rate-of-return drops significantly (e.g. Year 1's IRR is 55% and drops to 23% by Year 3). However, line **D** indicates a cumulative net cash generated of $61,936 by the end of Year 1 and $116,261 by the end of Year 3.

The total cash generated at the end of Year 3 has almost doubled. This is equivalent to a 37% return over a two-year period. Therefore, unless you have another investment opportunity that will yield a higher return than 37%, then you would probably not want to sell at the end of Year 1.

In this example, we also assumed that the tax losses were limited and no tax benefit was generated (as indicated in line **A**). As with most suspended passive losses, you do eventually receive the tax benefit upon the sale of the property. The tax benefit in this example is reflected in the property sale analysis as $40,711 (item **C**). Due to the short-term nature of the investment, the fact that the losses are suspended actually has an immaterial affect on the internal-rate-of-return.

Chapter 21

Sample Analysis #4 - Commercial Property

Commercial properties are evaluated differently than residential properties. Commercial properties are valued based on their cash flow and investment return rather than neighborhood comparables. Other differences include stepped rent increases rather than annual increases, the type of tenant, and the type of expenses incurred.

In Sample Analysis #4, we are evaluating a small commercial property with five units. We are using a 7.5% capitalization rate. The property is in relatively new condition and is listed for $455,000. The leases are locked for the next five years so there will be no revenue increase until the end of Year 5.

Asking Price:	$ 455,000
Capitalization Rate	7.5
Closing Costs	10,000
Future Commission on Sale	6%
Monthly Lease per Unit	1,250
Number of Units	5
Annual Lease Increase	0.0%
Expected Vacancy:	1 month out of 12, or 8%
Property Taxes	8,425
Insurance	4,950
Maintenance	3,500
Landscaping	5,400
Electricity	3,600
Water	2,895
Annual Increase in Expenses:	1%
Borrowing 80% for 30 years at:	8.50%
Marginal Tax Rates: Federal:	28.00%
Capital Gains:	15.00%
State Rate:	5.00%

5-Year Cash Flow Analysis

Rental Activity Analysis

	Year 3	Year 4	Year 5
Gross Rental Income	$ 75,000	$ 75,000	$ 75,000
Vacancy & Credits	(6,000)	(6,000)	(6,000)
Operating Expenses	(29,348)	(29,642)	(29,938)
Net Operating Income (NOI)	$ 39,652	$ 39,358	$ 39,062 ← **A**
Total Mortgage Payments	(34,324)	(34,324)	(34,324)
Operating Income Taxes: Benefit / (Expense)	315	315	308
Net CASH FLOW from Rent Activity	$ 5,642	$ 5,349	$ 5,046

Property Sale Analysis

	Year 3	Year 4	Year 5
Projected Sale Price	$ 528,690	$ 524,777	$ 520,824
Selling Expenses	(31,721)	(31,487)	(31,249)
Adjusted Projected Sales Price	496,968	493,290	489,575
Mortgage Balance Payoff	(363,084)	(359,484)	(355,568)
Income Taxes From Sale: Benefit / (Expense)	(14,905)	(17,046)	(19,180)
Net CASH FLOW from Property Sale	$ 118,979	$ 116,760	$ 114,830

Financial Ratios

	Year 3	Year 4	Year 5
Debt Coverage Ratio (DCR)	1.16	1.15	1.14 ← **B**
Capitalization Rate Based on Cost	8.53%	8.46%	8.40%
Capitalization Rate Based on FMV	7.50%	7.50%	7.50%
Value of Property Using This Cap Rate (8.50%)	466,491	463,038	459,551 ← **C**
Cash on Cash Return with Equity BuildUp	2.28%	2.21%	2.15%
Cash on Cash Return before Taxes	5.73%	5.41%	5.09%
Cash on Cash Return after Taxes	6.07%	5.75%	5.43%
Cumulative Internal Rate of Return (IRR)	15.19%	12.18%	10.41%
Modified Internal Rate of Return (MIRR)	14.47%	11.44%	9.68%

Based on the net operating income (line **A**), the value of the property is calculated to be $520,824 by the end of Year 5 ($39,062 / 7.5% capitalization rate.) As shown by line **C**, the software also allows us to evaluate the property at various capitalization rates for comparative purposes. At an 8.5% capitalization rate, the property is valued at $459,551 in Year 3.

As indicated by line **B**, the debt coverage ratio (DCR) is only 1.14. Since the net operating income is $39,062, we only have $4,738 remaining after paying the lender. This represents only 14% of the total mortgage payment. Lenders will prefer to see at least 20% or a 1.2 DCR. To obtain a DCR of 1.2, this property would need an additional $2,000 of NOI. Thus, we will probably have difficulty obtaining financing at the assumed 80% of cost.

The report below reflects a change from borrowing 80% of the cost to purchase to 75%.

5-Year Cash Flow Analysis
75% Financing

		Year 3	Year 4	Year 5	
Rental Activity Analysis					
Gross Rental Income	$	75,000	$ 75,000	$ 75,000	
Vacancy & Credits		(6,000)	(6,000)	(6,000)	
Operating Expenses		(29,348)	(29,642)	(29,938)	
Net Operating Income (NOI)	$	39,652	$ 39,358	$ 39,062	← A
Total Mortgage Payments		(32,179)	(32,179)	(32,179)	← B
Operating Income Taxes: Benefit / (Expense)		(325)	(318)	(319)	
Net CASH FLOW from Rent Activity	$	7,148	$ 6,861	$ 6,564	
Property Sale Analysis					
Projected Sale Price	$	528,690	$ 524,777	$ 520,824	
Selling Expenses		(31,721)	(31,487)	(31,249)	
Adjusted Projected Sales Price		496,968	493,290	489,575	
Mortgage Balance Payoff		(340,392)	(337,016)	(333,343)	
Income Taxes From Sale: Benefit / (Expense)		(14,905)	(17,046)	(19,180)	
Net CASH FLOW from Property Sale	$	141,672	$ 139,228	$ 137,052	

Financial Ratios					
Debt Coverage Ratio (DCR)		1.23	1.22	1.21	← C
Capitalization Rate Based on Cost		8.53%	8.46%	8.40%	
Capitalization Rate Based on FMV		7.50%	7.50%	7.50%	
Value of Property Using This Cap Rate	8.50%	466,491	463,038	459,551	
Cash on Cash Return with Equity BuildUp		2.89%	2.60%	2.52%	
Cash on Cash Return before Taxes		6.43%	6.18%	5.92%	
Cash on Cash Return after Taxes		6.15%	5.90%	5.65%	
Cumulative Internal Rate of Return (IRR)		13.36%	10.93%	9.50%	← D
Modified Internal Rate of Return (MIRR)		12.78%	10.32%	8.88%	

As indicated by line **B**, the loan payments are lower since we are not financing as much. Since our **NOI** in Year 5 (line **A**) remains the same, we now have $6,883 after debt payments (NOI of $39,062 less $32,179 debt payments). The excess now represents 21% of the debt payments, or a DCR of 1.21 (line **C**). However, while our lender may now sleep better at night, you may not. As indicated by line D, your internal rate-of-return went from 10.41% to 9.5% since you are leveraging less.

Section V: Real Estate Term Glossary

A

Abandonment
The voluntary relinquishment of rights of ownership or another form of interest (an easement) by failure to use the property over an extended period.

Abstract (Of Title)
A summary of the public records relating to the title to a particular piece of land. An attorney or title insurance company reviews an abstract of title to determine whether there are any title defects that must be cleared before a buyer can purchase clear, marketable, and insurable title.

Acceleration Clause
Condition in a mortgage that may require the balance of the loan to become due immediately. If regular mortgage payments are not made or there is a breach of other conditions, full payment of the mortgage will be due.

Acceptance
A legal term denoting acceptance of an offer. A buyer offers to buy and the seller accepts the offer.

Acknowledgment
A formal declaration by a person who has executed a document that he did, in fact, execute (sign) the document. An acknowledgement is signed in the presence of a notary public or other authorized official.

Acre
A measure of land equal to 160 sq. rods (43,560 sq. ft.). An acre is approximately 209' x 209'.

Addendums
Additions to a contract, sometimes called attachments or exhibits. Items added to a document, letter, contract, or escrow instructions, etc.

Adverse Possession
Method of acquiring title of a property by open and notorious possession. Laws vary from state to state.

Agency
(a) The relationship that exists when a person (known as the principal) contracts with another (the agent) to perform an act in that person's stead.
(b) Common term for a company offering representation.

Agency Disclosure
A state-mandated form that describes representation options available to the buyer that must be presented to all buyers at the first "meaningful meeting."

Agent
A person authorized by another to act on his or her behalf.

Agreement of Sale
Known by various names such as "contract of purchase," "purchase agreement," or "sales agreement" according to location or jurisdiction. A contract in which a seller agrees to sell and a buyer agrees to buy under certain specific terms and conditions -- spelled out in writing and signed by both parties.

Alienation Clause
A clause within a loan instrument requiring a debt to be paid in its entirety upon the transfer of ownership of the secured property. Also called a "due on sale" clause.

Amortization
A payment plan that enables the borrower to gradually reduce his debt through monthly payments of principal.

Amortization Schedule
A table that lists the percentage of each payment which consists of interest and principal.

Appraisal
An expert judgment or estimate of the quality or value of real estate as of a given date.

Asking Price
The price that a seller is requesting for his property, specified in a listing contract.

Assessed Value
Value placed on property by the tax assessor.

Assessment
The valuation of property for the purpose of levying a tax. An assessment also refers to the amount of tax levied.

Assessor
One appointed to assess property for taxation.

Assignment
A transfer of the whole of any property (real or personal) or of any estate or right therein. To assign is to transfer.

Assumption of Mortgage
An obligation undertaken by the purchaser of property to be personally liable for payment of an existing mortgage. In an assumption, the purchaser is substituted for the original mortgagor in the mortgage instrument, and the original mortgagor is released from further liability. In the assumption, the mortgagee's consent is usually required.

Attachment
Seizure of property by court order, usually done in a pending law suit to make property available in case of judgment.

B

Balloon Payment
The final installment paid at the end of the term of a note - used only when preceding installments were not sufficient to pay the note in full.

Bill of Sale
An instrument used to transfer personal property.

Binder or "Offer to Purchase"
A preliminary agreement that is secured by the payment of earnest money (between a buyer and seller) as an offer to purchase real estate. A binder secures the right to purchase real estate at agreed upon terms for a limited period of time. If the buyer changes his mind or is unable to purchase, the earnest money is forfeited unless the binder expressly provides that it is to be refunded.

Blanket Mortgage (Trust Deed)
A single mortgage or trust deed covering more than one piece of real estate.

Bond
(a). An insurance agreement by which one party is insured against loss or default by a third party. In the construction business, a performance bond ensures the interested party that the contractor will complete the project. (b) A method of financing debt by a government or corporation. A bond is interest bearing and has priority over stock in terms of security.

Breach
Violation of an obligation in a contract.

Broker, Real Estate
An agent licensed by the state to carry on the business of operating in real estate. He usually receives a commission for bringing together buyers and sellers or owners and tenants in exchange agreements.

Broker's Commission
A section of the "offer to purchase" and the "purchase and sale agreement" outlining the real estate broker's fees.

Building Code
A set of stringent laws that control the construction of buildings, design, materials, and other similar factors.

Built-Ins
Items that are not movable, such as stoves, ovens, microwave ovens, or dishwashers.

Buyer Broker
A real estate agent who specializes in representing the purchaser. Some agents who specialize in this area are referred to as Exclusive Buyers Agents and do not list properties. Most real estate agents throughout the USA and Canada work with many of the more commonly known franchises to list and sell property.

Buyers Market
A market condition that occurs in real estate when more homes are for sale than there are interested buyers.

C

Capital Cost Allowance
Decline in value of a house due to wear and tear and/or adverse changes in the neighborhood or any other reason.

Capital Gains
A term used for income tax purposes that represents the gain realized from the sale of an asset less the purchase price.

Capitalization
An appraising term used in determining value by considering net operating income and a percentage of reasonable return-on-investment.

Cash Flow
The owner's "spendable" income after operating expenses and debt service is deducted.

CCIM
The highest designation of commercial specialists is the CCIM, Certified Commercial Investment Member, conferred by the Commercial Investment Real Estate Institute of NAR.

Certificate of Title
A certificate issued by a title company or a written opinion rendered by an attorney that the seller has good marketable and insurable title to the property that he is offering for sale. A certificate of title offers no protection against any hidden defects in the title that an examination of the records could not reveal. The issuer of a certificate of title is liable only for damages due to negligence. The protection offered a homeowner under a certificate of title is not as great as that offered in a title insurance policy.

Chain Of Title
A history of conveyances and encumbrances affecting the title as far back as records are available.

Closing
In the sale of real estate, it is the final moment when all documents are executed and recorded, and the sale is complete

Closing Costs
The expenses which buyers and sellers normally incur to complete a transaction in the transfer of ownership of real estate. These costs are in addition to the price of the property and are items paid at closing.

Closing Date
The date on which the title to the property changes hands.

Closing Statement
A list of the final accounting of all funds and disbursements of both the buyer and seller. The closing statement is usually given at the completion of a real estate transaction.

CMA - See Comparative Market Analysis

Code of Ethics
The rules and regulations required by all members of the National Association of Realtors.

Commission
Money paid to a real estate agent or broker by the seller as compensation for finding a buyer and completing the sale. Usually it is a percentage of the sale price (6 to 7 percent on houses, 10 percent on land.).

Commitment Letter
A letter from the lending institution giving formal approval for a mortgage loan.

Common Area
That area owned in common by owners of condominiums and planned site development homes within a subdivision.

Community Property
Both real and personal property accumulated by a husband and wife after marriage through joint efforts of both living together.

Comparative Market Analysis (CMA)
A service normally provided by real estate agents prior to either listing a property or to making an offer to purchase a property on the behalf of a purchaser. The true purpose of a CMA is to establish a current estimated market price of a property. This is accomplished by researching both the currently listed properties and the most recently sold properties, in the same area, with similar characteristics to the property in question. This information is usually provided to homeowners to help them establish a fair market selling price; it may also be given to a prospective purchaser to help guide them in making a proper offer. Some real estate agents perform this service for free while others may charge as much as $300 for this information.

Condemnation
A declaration by governing powers that a structure is unfit for use.

Conditional Sales Contract
A contract for the sale of property gives the buyer possession and use, but the seller retains title until the conditions of the contract have been fulfilled. Also known as a land contract.

Condominium
Individual ownership of a dwelling unit and an individual interest in the common areas and facilities that serve the multi-unit project.

Consideration
Anything of value given to induce someone into entering into a contract.

Construction Loan
The short-term financing of improvements on real estate. Once the improvements are completed, a "take out" loan for a longer term is usually issued.

Contingency
A condition upon which a valid contract is dependent. Typically found in the "offer to purchase" and the "purchase and sale agreement." For example, the sale of a house is contingent upon the buyer obtaining adequate financing.

Contract
An agreement between two or more parties, written or oral, to do or not to do certain things.

Contractor
In the construction industry, a contractor is one who contracts to erect buildings or portions of them. There are also contractors for each phase of construction - heating, electrical, plumbing, air conditioning, road building, bridge and dam erection, and others.

Conventional Mortgage
A mortgage loan not insured by HUD or guaranteed by the Veterans' Administration. Subject to conditions established by the lending institution and state statutes. The mortgage rates may vary with different institutions and between states. (States have various interest rate limits)

Conveyance
The transfer of title to land from one owner to the next.

Co-Op Housing
An apartment building or a group of dwellings owned by a corporation; the stockholders are the residents of the dwellings. It is operated for their benefit by their elected board of directors. In a cooperative, the corporation or association owns title to the real estate. A resident purchases stock in the corporation that entitles him to occupy a unit in the building or property owned by the cooperative. While the resident does not own his unit, he has an absolute right to occupy his unit for as long as he owns the stock.

Counter Offer
An offer in response to an offer. A offers to by B's house for $20,000, which is listed for $22,000. 'B' counter offers 'A's' offer by stating that he will sell the house to 'A" for $21,000. The $21,000 is the counter offer.

Covenants
Agreements written into deeds and other instruments stating performance or non-performance of certain acts or noting certain uses or non-uses of property.

Credit Report
A report on a buyer's credit history required by the lender before approval of a loan.

Credit Score
A potential borrower's composite of available credit, outstanding credit, and payment history.

D

Debt Service
The total amount of the loan payment including principal and interest.

Deed
A formal written instrument by which title to real property is transferred from one owner to another. The deed should contain an accurate description of the property being conveyed, should be signed and witnessed according to the laws of the state where the property is located, and should be delivered to the purchaser at closing. There are two parties to a deed, the grantor and the grantee. (See also deed of trust, general warranty deed, quitclaim deed, and special warranty deed.)

Default
Failure to make mortgage payments as agreed in a contract based on the terms and at the designated time set forth in the mortgage or deed of trust. It is the mortgagor's responsibility to remember the due date and send the payment prior to the due date, not after. In the event of default, the mortgage may give the lender the right to accelerate payments, take possession and receive rents, and start foreclosure. Defaults may also result from the failure to observe other conditions in the mortgage or deed of trust.

Down Payment
The amount of money to be paid by the purchaser to the seller upon the signing of the agreement of sale. The agreement of sale specifies the down payment amount and will acknowledge receipt of the down-payment. The down payment is the difference between the sales price and maximum mortgage amount. The down payment may not be refundable if the purchaser fails to buy the property without good cause. If the purchaser wants the down payment to be refundable, he should insert a clause in the agreement of sale, specifying the conditions under which the deposit will be refunded, if the agreement does not already

contain such clause. If the seller cannot deliver good title, the agreement of sale usually requires the seller to return the down payment and to pay interest and expenses incurred by the purchaser.

E

Earnest Money
The deposit money given to the seller or his agent by the potential buyer upon the signing of the "agreement of sale" to show that he is serious about buying the house. If the sale is transacted, the earnest money is applied against the down-payment. If the sale falls through, the earnest money will be forfeited or lost unless the binder or offer to purchase expressly provides that it is refundable.

Easement Rights
A right-of-way granted to a person or company authorizing access to or over the owner's land. An electric company obtaining a right-of-way across private property is a common example.

Economic Obsolescence
Loss of useful life and desirability of a property through economic forces, such as change in zoning, changes in traffic flow, etc. -- rather than deterioration.

Encroachment
An obstruction, building, or part of a building that intrudes beyond a legal boundary onto neighboring private or public land.

Encumbrance
A legal right or interest in land that affects a good or clear title and diminishes the lands value. It can take numerous forms, such as zoning ordinances, easement rights, claims, mortgages, liens, charges, a pending legal action, unpaid taxes, or restrictive covenants. An encumbrance does not legally prevent transfer of the property to another. A title search is all that is usually done to reveal the existence of such encumbrances. The buyer must decide if he wants to purchase with the encumbrance or find out what can be done to remove it.

Equity
The value of a homeowner's unencumbered interest in real estate. Equity is computed by subtracting the property's fair market value from the total of the unpaid mortgage balance and any outstanding liens or other debts against the property. A homeowner's equity increases as he pays off his mortgage or as the property appreciates in value. When the mortgage and all the debts against the property are paid in full, the homeowner has 100% equity in his property.

Escalation Clause
A clause in a lease providing for an increased rent at a future time due to increased costs to lessor, as in cost of living index, tax increases, etc.

Escheat
The reverting of property to the state in the absence of heirs.

Escrow
Funds paid by one party to another (the escrow agent) to hold until the occurrence of a specified event, after which the funds are released to a designated individual. In FHA mortgage transactions an escrow account usually refers to the funds a mortgagor pays the lender at the time of the periodic mortgage payments. The money is held in a trust fund for the buyer. Such funds should be adequate to cover yearly anticipated expenditures for mortgage insurance premiums, taxes, hazard insurance premiums, and special assessments.

Escrow Account
(a) An account maintained by a real estate broker, attorney, or escrow agent in an insured bank for the deposit of other people's money. (b) An account maintained by the borrower with the lender in certain mortgage loans used to accumulate the funds to pay annual insurance premiums, real estate taxes, or home owner's association assessments.

Estate
The ownership interest of a person in real property. Is also used to refer to a deceased person's property. Estate is also a term used to describe a large home with spacious grounds.

Exclusions
A section of the "offer to purchase agreement" designed to exhibit anything the buyer or seller would not like included with the real estate (i.e. rusted swing set in yard).

Exclusive Buyer Representation
An agency relationship between a buyer and a broker that cannot result in dual agency.

Executed Contract
An agreement that has been fully performed.

Expiration Date and Time
A section of the "offer to purchase agreement" designed to give the offer a time limit after which the offer is withdrawn.

Extensions
Written or verbal extensions of dates in the "offer to purchase" and the "purchase and sale agreement."

F

Fair Market Value
That price a property will bring between a willing buyer and a willing seller.

Fee Simple
Ownership of title to property without any limitation that can be sold, left at will, or inherited.

Fiduciary Duties
An obligation of trust imposed on an agent toward his/her principal. These duties include loyalty, disclosure, confidentiality, obedience, reasonable care, due diligence, and accountability for funds and documents under the agent's control. Every agent has a fiduciary responsibility to the principal, once they are engaged.

Financing Acceptance Deadline
The date in the "offer to purchase agreement" that the buyer expects to have the loan commitment from the bank. This deadline may be used to nullify the sales contract if the mortgage is not obtained.

Fixed Rate Loan
A loan that has an unchanging interest rate.

Fixtures
Items affixed to buildings or land usually in such a way that they cannot be moved without damage to themselves or the property, such as plumbing, electrical fixtures, trees, etc.

Foreclosure
A legal term applied to any of the various methods of enforcing payment of the debt secured by a mortgage or deed of trust by taking and selling the mortgaged property and depriving the mortgagor of possession.

Front Footage
The linear measurement along the front of a parcel. That portion of the parcel that fronts the street or walkway.

FSBO (For Sale By Owner)
A home that is being sold by the owner of the property without the representation of a broker.

Functional Obsolescence
Loss in value due to out-of-date or poorly designed equipment due to the invention of newer equipment and structures..

G

General Warranty Deed
A deed which conveys not only all the grantor's interests in and the title to the property to the grantee, but also warrants that if the title is defective, such as mortgage claims, tax liens, title claims, judgments, or mechanic's liens against it, the grantee may hold the grantor liable.

Good Faith Estimate
A required statement from the lender that shows all of the expected closing costs.

Grantee
That party in the deed that is the buyer or recipient.

Grantor
That party in the deed that is the seller or giver.

Ground Lease
A lease of vacant land

H

Hard Credit Report
A report on one's credit history that is a compilation of the three credit bureaus.

Hazard Insurance
Protects against damages caused to property by fire, windstorms, and other common hazards.

Home Owners Association
An association of homeowners within a community formed to improve and maintain the quality of the community. An association formed by the developer of condominiums or planned developments.

HUD
U.S. Department of Housing and Urban Development. Office of housing/Federal Housing Administration within HUD insures home mortgage loans made by lenders and sets minimum standards for such homes.

I

Inclusions
A section of the offer to purchase designed to exhibit any extra items the buyer or seller would like to be included with the real estate (i.e. personal property).

Inspections
The analysis of the home to find any defects that may exist.

Interest
Money paid to a lender as compensation for money that is borrowed.

Involuntary Lien
A lien that attaches to property without the consent of the owner such as a tax or mechanic's lien.

J

Joint Tenancy
Joint ownership by two or more persons with right of survivorship. Upon the death of a joint tenant, his interest does not go to his heirs but to the remaining joint tenants.

L

Lease
A contract between the owner of real property, called the lessor, and another person referred to as the lessee, covering all conditions by which the lessee may occupy and use the property.

Lease with Option to Purchase
A lease which allows the lessee the option to purchase the leased property. The terms of the purchase option must be set forth in the lease.

Legal Description
The geographical identification of a parcel of land.

Lessee
One who contracts to rent property under a specified lease.

Lessor
An owner who contracts into a lease with a tenant (lessee).

Lien
A claim by one person on the property of another as security for money owed. Such claims may include obligations not met such as judgments, unpaid taxes, materials, or labor. (See also Special Lien.)

Life Estate
An estate in real property for the life of a person

Listing
(a) A property included in the multiple listing service. (b) A written agreement between a seller and a broker authorizing the broker to procure a buyer or tenant for his/her real estate.

Listing Agent
The broker employed by a principal to market a property.

Living Trust
A trust agreement into which the title to property and assets can be transferred to avoid probate. A Trust is created when a living person (the Trustor) agrees to let someone (the Trustee) hold title to property for the benefit of someone (the Beneficiary).

Loan Fee
Also known as points, discount points or origination fee, this is a one time charge by a lender as compensation for their services. One point equals 1% of the mortgage amount.

Loan Originator
A person who works for the lending institution whose job it is to meet with potential borrowers to discuss loan options, rates, etc.

M

Market Analysis
An analysis performed to determine the current value of a property based on recently sold comparable properties, comparable properties that are currently for sale and the current overall market conditions.

Marketable Title
A title that is free and clear of objectionable liens or other title defects. A title that enables an owner to sell his property freely to others and one which others will accept without objection.

Mechanic's Lien
A lien on a specific property for labor or materials used to improve the property. Generally filed by a contractor when the homeowner does not

pay for the labor and materials used for improving the homeowner's property.

Mortgage
A legal document that pledges property to a creditor for the repayment of the loan, as well as the term used to describe the loan itself. Some states use the term First Trust Deeds to refer to mortgage loans.

Mortgage Commitment
A written commitment from the lending institution to provide a mortgage to the buyer for a specific property.

Mortgage Contingency
A contingency in the offer to purchase and/or the purchase and sale agreement which protects the buyers in case they are unable to get a mortgage by the commitment date specified in the contract.

Mortgagee
The lender in a mortgage agreement.

Mortgagor
The borrower in a mortgage agreement.

Multiple Listing
A listing of a property for sale by an organization of brokers whereby all members of the organization have an opportunity to sell the property.

Multiple Listing Service
A service provided to real estate agents that lists homes under a seller's representation agreement and may be available for sale. A computerized database of all homes listed by real estate agents.

N

Notary Public
One who is authorized by federal or local government to attest to authentic signatures and administer oaths.

Note
A written instrument acknowledging a debt and promising payment.

O

Offer
A presentation to form a contract or agreement to buy or sell an property.

Offer to Purchase Agreement
The agreement between a buyer and seller for a specified price and terms or conditions.

Option
A right given, for consideration, to purchase or lease property upon stipulated terms within a specific period of time.

Origination Fee
Application fee(s) imposed by a lender for processing a proposed mortgage.

P

Personal Property
All property that is not land and is not permanently attached to land; everything that is movable.

PITI
Principal, interest, taxes, and insurance. This is your monthly mortgage payment.

Plot
A map or chart of a lot, subdivision, or community drawn by a surveyor showing boundary lines, buildings, improvements on the land, and easements.

PMI – See Private Mortgage Insurance

Points
Sometimes called "discount points. " A point is one percent of the amount of the mortgage loan. For example, if a loan is for $25,000, one point is equal to $250. Points are charged by a lender to raise the yield on his loan at a time when money is tight, interest rates are high, and there is a legal limit to the interest rate that can be charged on a mortgage. Buyers are prohibited from paying points on HUD or Veterans' Administration guaranteed loans (sellers can pay, however). On a conventional mortgage, points may be paid by either buyer or seller or split between them.

Pre-approval
A pre-commitment from a lending institution to a buyer based on background checks, hard credit reports, and review by an underwriter.

Prepayment
Payment of mortgage loan, or part of it, before the due date. Mortgage agreements sometimes restrict the right of prepayment either by limiting

the amount that can be prepaid in any one year or charging a penalty for prepayment.

Prepayment Penalty
A penalty within a note, mortgage, or deed of trust imposing a penalty if the debt is paid in full before the end of its terms.

Pre-qualifying
The lender's process of judging if a borrower is creditworthy and capable of making payments on a loan.

Principal
The basic element of the loan as distinguished from interest and mortgage insurance premium. In other words, principal is the amount upon which interest is paid.

Private Mortgage Insurance (PMI)
A type of insurance required by many lenders when a borrower's down payment is less then 20% of the purchase price.

Promissory Note
A written promise to pay a debt.

Property Tax and Insurance Escrow
Money collected monthly by the lender and held to pay taxes and insurance when due.

Purchase and Sale Agreement
Detailed document(s) regarding the agreement between the buyer and seller on the price and other terms and conditions of the transaction written in "legalese."

R

Real Estate
Land and everything permanently attached to the land, sometimes used interchangeably with the terms real property and realty.

Real Estate Agent
A licensed person who works under the direction of a broker selling and renting real estate.

Real Estate Broker
(a) A person or organization who negotiates real estate sales, exchanges, or remittals for others for compensation or a promise of compensation.
(b) Supervisor of real estate salespeople.

Real Estate Salesperson
A person performing any of the acts included in the definition of real estate broker but while associated with and supervised by a real estate broker.

Realtor
A real estate broker holding membership in a real estate board affiliated with the National Association of Realtors.

Recording Deed
Entering the deed (owner's title) in public records to protect against subsequent claimants.

Refinancing
The process of the same mortgagor paying off one loan with the proceeds from another loan.

Representation Agreement
A mutual contractual agreement between the agency and the client committing services and fiduciary duties to the client.

Restrictive Covenants
Private restrictions limiting the use of real property. Restrictive covenants are created by deed and may "run with the land," binding all subsequent purchasers of the land, or may be "personal" and binding only between the original seller and buyer. The determination whether a covenant runs with the land or is personal is governed by the language of the covenant, the intent of the parties, and the law in the state where the land is situated. Restrictive covenants that run with the land are encumbrances and may affect the value and marketability of title. Restrictive covenants may limit the density of buildings per acre, regulate size, style or price range of buildings to be erected, or prevent particular businesses from operating or minority groups from owning or occupying homes in a given area.

RREI

Residential Real Estate Inspector (RREI) or Commercial Real Estate Inspector (CREI) are both members of the Foundation of Real Estate Appraisers (FREA).

S

Sales Agreement - See Agreement of Sale.

Seller Representation
Offered by firms representing sellers (might offer buyer representation as well)

Seller's Market
A market condition when there are more interested buyers than there are properties for sale.

Setback
The distance from the front or interior property line to the point where a structure can be located.

Smoke Detector Certificate
Written verification from a municipality that the smoke detectors in a home meet the necessary standards.

Soft Credit Report
A report on one's credit history from one of the credit bureaus.

Special Assessments
A special tax imposed on property, individual lots, or all property in the immediate area, for road construction, sidewalks, sewers, street lights, etc.

Special Conditions
A section of the "offer to purchase agreement" designed to exhibit any special circumstances, contingencies or addendums desired by the buyer or seller.

Special Lien
A lien that binds a specified piece of property, unlike a general lien, which is levied against all one's assets. It creates a right to retain something of value belonging to another person as compensation for labor, material, or money expended in that person's behalf. In some localities it is called "particular" lien or "specific" lien. (See Lien)

Special Warranty Deed
A deed in which the grantor conveys title to the grantee and agrees to protect the grantee against title defects or claims asserted by the grantor and those persons whose right to assert a claim against the title arose during the period the grantor held title to the property. In a special warranty deed, the grantor guarantees to the grantee that he has done nothing that has impaired the grantee's title during the time he held title to the property.

Sub-agent
A real estate agent working for a principal through another real estate agent or agency.

Survey
A map or plot made by a licensed surveyor showing the results of measuring the land with its elevations, improvements, boundaries, and its relationship to surrounding tracts of land. A survey is often required by the lender to assure him that a building is actually sited on the land according to its legal description.

T

Tax
A fee or levy imposed on persons, property or income by a government agency.

Term
The length of time in which a loan is to be paid off.

Terms and Conditions
The negotiable issues outlined in the "offer to purchase agreement" and the "purchase and sale agreement."

Title
A document establishing ownership of a specific parcel of real estate.

Title Insurance
Protects lenders or homeowners against loss of their interest in property due to legal defects in title.

Title V Examination
A test put together by the state EPA that must be performed on all private sewerage systems.

Title Search or Examination
A check of the title records, generally at the local courthouse, to make sure the buyer is purchasing a house from the legal owner and there are no liens, overdue special assessments, or other claims or outstanding restrictive covenants filed in the record that would adversely affect the marketability or value of title.

Trustee
A party who is given legal responsibility to hold property in the best interest of or "for the benefit of" another. The trustee is one that is placed in a position of responsibility for another, a responsibility enforceable in a court of law.

U

Underwriter
The person in the lending institution whose job it is to review loan documentation and evaluate the borrower's ability and willingness to repay the loan.

Undisclosed Dual Agency
An illegal situation that arises when a real estate broker represents both parties but does not inform one or more of the parties.

V

Variable Interest Rate
A fluctuating interest rate that can go up or down depending on the going market rate.

Voluntary Lien
A voluntary lien by the owner such as a mortgage, as opposed to involuntary liens (taxes).

W

Waive
To relinquish, or abandon. To forego a right to enforce or require anything.

Walk-through
A final inspection of the property before closing to see that all agreed to repairs, etc. have been completed and that the property is in the condition the buyer expects.

Warranties and Representations
A section of the "offer to purchase agreement" designed to exhibit representations or warranties made by the real estate brokers or the seller.

Wrap-Around Mortgage
A second mortgage that is subordinate to but includes the face value of the first mortgage.

Z

Zoning Ordinances
The acts of an authorized local government establishing building codes and setting forth regulations for property land usage.

Section VI: Appendices
Appendix 1

Input Data Sheets and Other Reports for Sample Analysis #1

Input Data Screen

Property Name: Sample Analysis #1
Case Description:
Address:
Address:

[Sensitivity Analysis] [Executive Report]
[Main Report] [User Guide]
[Graphs & Reports] [APOD Report]

I. Rental Income & Expenses

Rental Income / Rent Roll:	[Enter Rent Roll]
Operating Expenses:	[Enter Expenses]
Enter Average Vacancy Rate:	4.20%
Annual Rental Income Growth Rate (%) [Enter Annual Rates] Apply This Rate Every Year ==>	2.00%
Annual Operating Expense Increase (%):	2.00%

II. Property Costs & Characteristics

Select Residential, Commercial Property or Raw Land		Single-Family
Number of Units / Total Square Footage of Property	1	1,500

Purchase Price of Rental Property:		
Contract Purchase Price	$	105,000
Initial Improvements	$	-
Closing Costs	$	750
Other Initial Costs		-
Enter 5-Year Personal Property ==>	$	-
% of Cost Allocated to Land	20.00%	$ 105,750 <== Total Cost

Current Fair Market Value (FMV) of Rental Property:	$	105,750
Annual Appreciation Rate (%): [Enter Annual Rates] Apply This Rate Every Year ==>		3.50%
Future Selling Expenses (as a % of Selling Price):		6.00%

	Description	Amount	Select Year Improvement to be Made	Will the improvement increase the property's FMV?
Future Property		$ -	4	No
Improvements		$ -	2	No
		$ -	2	No
Total		$ -		

III. Financing [Amort Schedules]

	Mortgage #1	Mortgage #2	Mortgage #3
Amount **Borrowed** or **Assumed**:	$ 84,600	$ -	$ -
Interest Rate:	7.250%	[Enter Loan Rate]	[Enter Loan Rate]
Interest Only?	No	No	No
Enter **Start Month** of the Loan:	Month 1	Month 1	Month 1
Enter **Start Year** of the Loan:	Year 1	Year 1	Year 1
Term / Remaining Term of Loan (**In Months**):	360	360	360
Is this to Refinance Mortgage #1 or #2	n/a	No - New Loan	No - New Loan
Additional Monthly Principal Payments	-	-	-
Monthly Mortgage Payment (Formula)	$ 577.12	$ -	$ -
Loan Origination **Points**	-	-	-
Loan Origination Points (In Dollars)	$ -	$ -	$ -

Initial Investment or Down Payment (Cost less Debt - Automatically Calculated)	$	21,150
Down Payment as a Percent of Fair Market Value		20.0%
Down Payment as a Percent of Cost		20.0%

IV. Income Taxes

Federal Marginal Income Tax Rate:	28.0%
Federal Long-Term Capital Gains Rate:	15%
State Marginal Income Tax Rate:	5%
Are Your Losses Limited by the Passive Loss Rules?	No
Like-Kind Exchange on Disposition?	No

Rental Income / Rent Roll

Enter Lease Description	Monthly Rent	Vacant / Incentive Months in the First Year
Unit 1	$ 1,050	0
Unit 2	$ -	0
Unit 3	$ -	0
Unit 4	$ -	0
Unit 5	$ -	0
Unit 6	$ -	0
Unit 7	$ -	0
Unit 8	$ -	0
Unit 9	$ -	0
Unit 10	$ -	0

Annual Rental Expense Input Screen

Total Annual Expenses:	$	5,025	(from below)
Annual Increase		2.00%	(from Input Screen)
Monthly Expenses	$	419	$ -

Expense Description	Annual Amount	Percentage of Total
Accounting	$ -	0.00%
Advertising	$ -	0.00%
Association Fees	$ -	0.00%
Auto & Travel	$ -	0.00%
Cleaning	$ -	0.00%
Commissions	$ -	0.00%
Insurance	$ 1,100	21.89%
Lawn Maintenance	$ -	0.00%
Legal	$ -	0.00%
Maintenance	$ 1,500	29.85%
Other	$ -	0.00%
Payroll	$ -	0.00%
Professional Fees	$ -	0.00%
Repairs	$ -	0.00%
Supplies	$ -	0.00%
Taxes:		
Property Taxes	$ 2,425	48.26%
Personal Property	$ -	0.00%
Payroll	$ -	0.00%
Other	$ -	0.00%
Trash Removal	$ -	0.00%
Utilities:		
Electricity	$ -	0.00%
Water	$ -	0.00%
Gas	$ -	0.00%
Telephone	$ -	0.00%
Other Utilities	$ -	0.00%
Miscellaneous	$ -	0.00%
Miscellaneous	$ -	0.00%
Miscellaneous	$ -	0.00%
Miscellaneous	$ -	0.00%
Miscellaneous	$ -	0.00%
Total Annual Expenses	$ 5,025	

Mortgage 1

Principal	84,600
Rate	7.25%
Term	360
Payment	$ 577.12

Month	Balance	Principal	Interest	Payment	Principal Year	Interest: Year
1	84,600	66	511	577		
2	84,534	66	511	577		
3	84,468	67	510	577		
4	84,401	67	510	577		
5	84,334	68	510	577		
6	84,266	68	509	577		
7	84,198	68	509	577		
8	84,130	69	508	577		
9	84,061	69	508	577		
10	83,991	70	507	577		
11	83,922	70	507	577	748	5,600
12	83,852	71	507	577		
13	83,781	71	506	577		
14	83,710	71	506	577		
15	83,639	72	505	577		
16	83,567	72	505	577		
17	83,495	73	504	577		
18	83,422	73	504	577		
19	83,349	74	504	577		
20	83,276	74	503	577		
21	83,202	74	503	577		
22	83,127	75	502	577		
23	83,052	75	502	577	875	6,051

Annual Property Cash Flow - 20 Year Projection

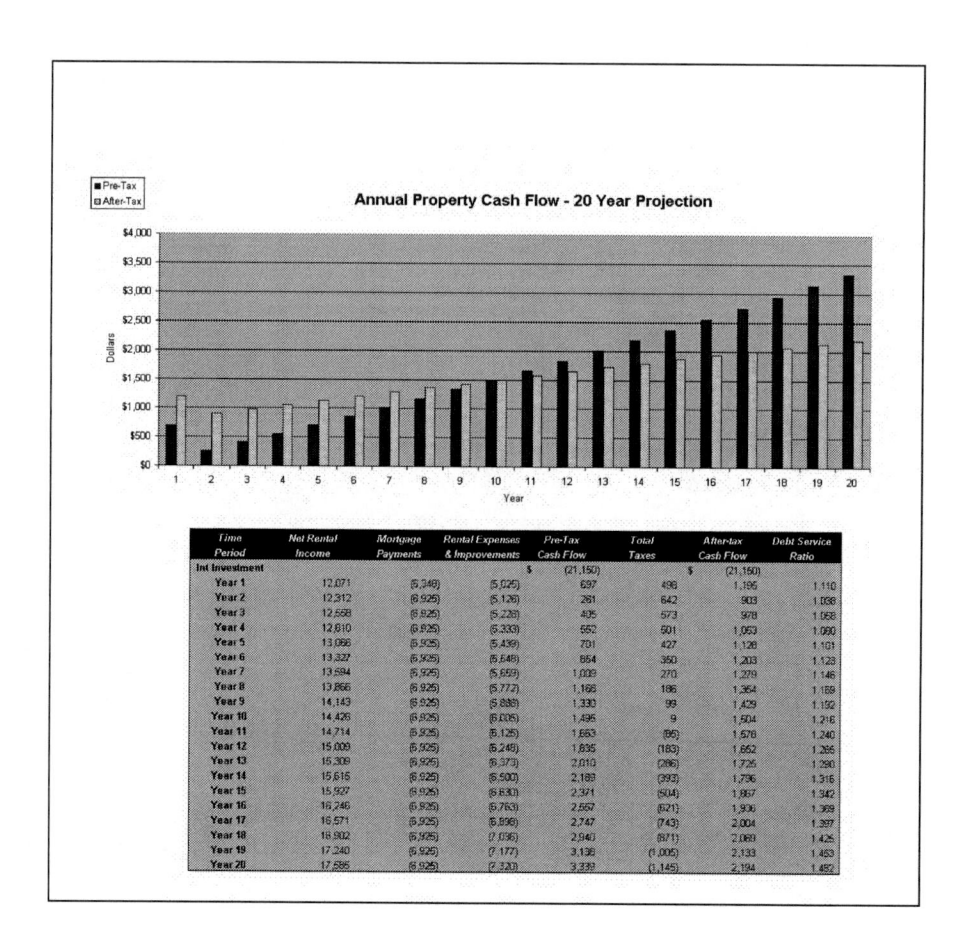

■ Pre-Tax
□ After-Tax

Time Period	Net Rental Income	Mortgage Payments	Rental Expenses & Improvements	Pre-Tax Cash Flow	Total Taxes	After-tax Cash Flow	Debt Service Ratio
Init Investment				$ (21,150)		$ (21,150)	
Year 1	12,071	(5,348)	(5,025)	697	498	1,195	1.110
Year 2	12,312	(6,925)	(5,126)	261	642	903	1.038
Year 3	12,558	(6,925)	(5,228)	405	573	978	1.058
Year 4	12,810	(6,925)	(5,333)	552	501	1,053	1.080
Year 5	13,066	(6,925)	(5,439)	701	427	1,128	1.101
Year 6	13,327	(6,925)	(5,548)	854	350	1,203	1.123
Year 7	13,594	(6,925)	(5,659)	1,009	270	1,279	1.146
Year 8	13,866	(6,925)	(5,772)	1,168	186	1,354	1.169
Year 9	14,143	(6,925)	(5,888)	1,330	99	1,429	1.192
Year 10	14,426	(6,925)	(6,005)	1,495	9	1,504	1.216
Year 11	14,714	(6,925)	(6,125)	1,663	(95)	1,578	1.240
Year 12	15,009	(6,925)	(6,248)	1,835	(183)	1,652	1.265
Year 13	15,309	(6,925)	(6,373)	2,010	(286)	1,725	1.290
Year 14	15,615	(6,925)	(6,500)	2,189	(392)	1,796	1.316
Year 15	15,927	(6,925)	(6,630)	2,371	(504)	1,867	1.342
Year 16	16,246	(6,925)	(6,763)	2,557	(621)	1,936	1.369
Year 17	16,571	(6,925)	(6,898)	2,747	(743)	2,004	1.397
Year 18	16,902	(6,925)	(7,036)	2,940	(871)	2,069	1.425
Year 19	17,240	(6,925)	(7,177)	3,138	(1,005)	2,133	1.453
Year 20	17,585	(6,925)	(7,320)	3,339	(1,145)	2,194	1.482

102

Cash on Cash Return

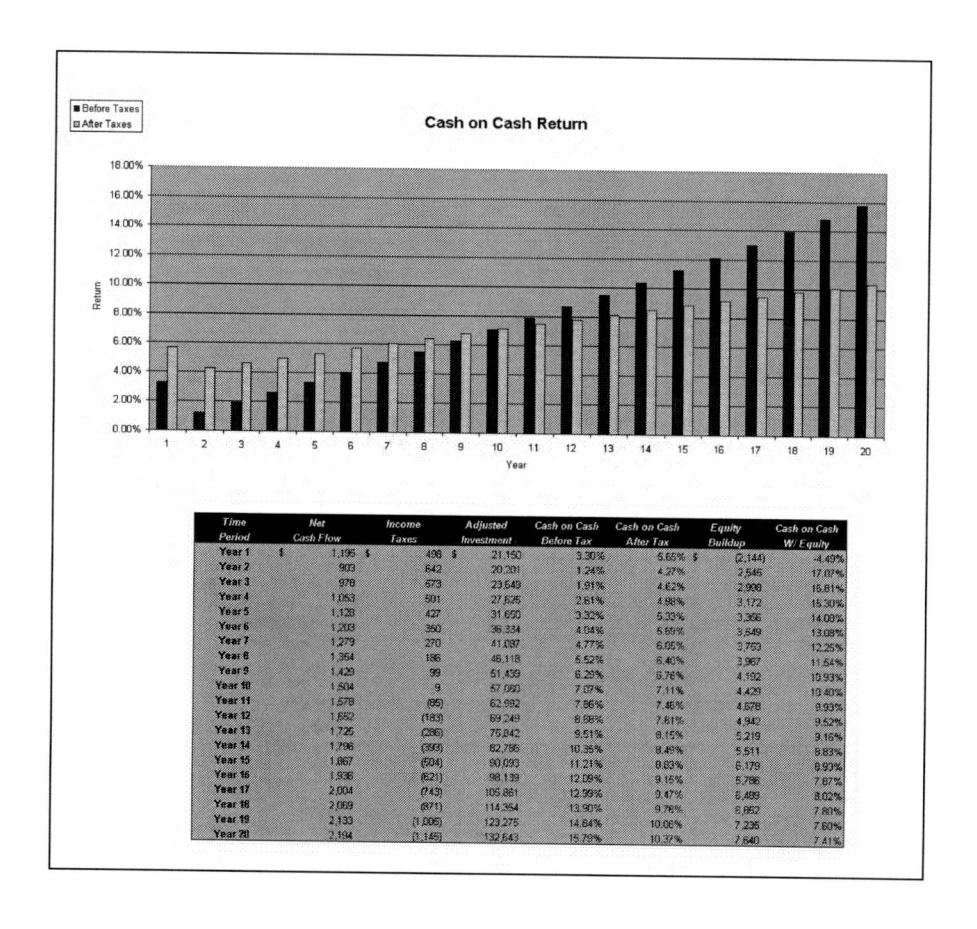

Time Period	Net Cash Flow	Income Taxes	Adjusted Investment	Cash on Cash Before Tax	Cash on Cash After Tax	Equity Buildup	Cash on Cash W/ Equity
Year 1	$ 1,196	$ 496	$ 21,150	3.30%	5.65%	$ (2,144)	-4.49%
Year 2	903	542	20,391	1.24%	4.27%	2,545	17.07%
Year 3	978	573	23,549	1.91%	4.62%	2,998	15.81%
Year 4	1,053	501	27,625	2.61%	4.98%	3,172	15.30%
Year 5	1,128	427	31,650	3.32%	5.33%	3,356	14.09%
Year 6	1,203	350	36,334	4.04%	5.69%	3,549	13.08%
Year 7	1,279	270	41,097	4.77%	6.05%	3,753	12.25%
Year 8	1,354	186	46,118	5.52%	6.40%	3,967	11.54%
Year 9	1,429	99	51,459	6.29%	6.76%	4,192	10.93%
Year 10	1,504	9	57,060	7.07%	7.11%	4,429	10.40%
Year 11	1,578	(85)	62,982	7.86%	7.46%	4,678	9.93%
Year 12	1,652	(183)	69,249	8.66%	7.81%	4,942	9.52%
Year 13	1,725	(286)	75,842	9.51%	8.15%	5,219	9.16%
Year 14	1,796	(395)	82,795	10.35%	8.48%	5,511	8.83%
Year 15	1,867	(504)	90,090	11.21%	8.83%	6,179	8.90%
Year 16	1,936	(621)	98,139	12.09%	9.16%	5,786	7.67%
Year 17	2,004	(743)	105,861	12.99%	9.47%	6,499	8.02%
Year 18	2,069	(871)	114,354	13.90%	9.76%	6,852	7.80%
Year 19	2,133	(1,005)	123,275	14.84%	10.06%	7,235	7.60%
Year 20	2,194	(1,145)	132,643	15.79%	10.37%	7,640	7.41%

Capitalization Rate

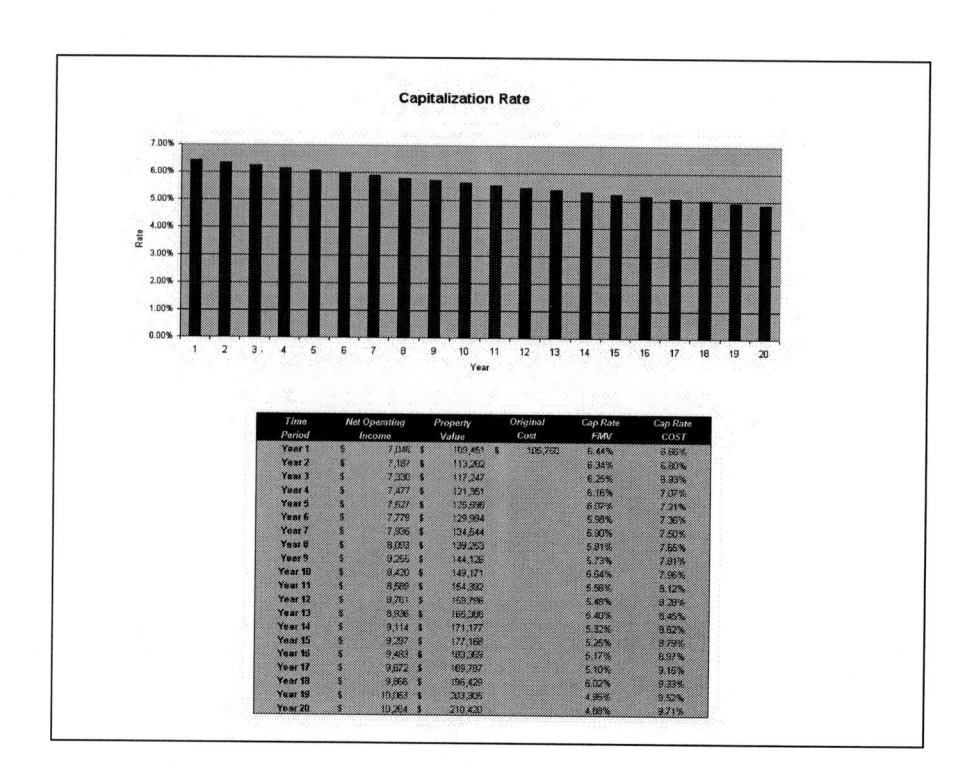

Time Period	Net Operating Income	Property Value	Original Cost	Cap Rate FMV	Cap Rate COST
Year 1	$ 7,046	$ 109,451	$ 105,750	6.44%	6.66%
Year 2	$ 7,187	$ 113,262		6.34%	6.80%
Year 3	$ 7,330	$ 117,247		6.25%	6.93%
Year 4	$ 7,477	$ 121,351		6.16%	7.07%
Year 5	$ 7,627	$ 125,696		6.07%	7.21%
Year 6	$ 7,779	$ 129,994		5.98%	7.36%
Year 7	$ 7,935	$ 134,544		5.90%	7.50%
Year 8	$ 8,093	$ 139,253		5.81%	7.65%
Year 9	$ 8,255	$ 144,126		5.73%	7.81%
Year 10	$ 8,420	$ 149,171		5.64%	7.96%
Year 11	$ 8,589	$ 154,392		5.56%	8.12%
Year 12	$ 8,761	$ 159,796		5.48%	8.28%
Year 13	$ 8,936	$ 165,389		5.40%	8.45%
Year 14	$ 9,114	$ 171,177		5.32%	8.62%
Year 15	$ 9,297	$ 177,168		5.25%	8.79%
Year 16	$ 9,483	$ 183,369		5.17%	8.97%
Year 17	$ 9,672	$ 189,787		5.10%	9.15%
Year 18	$ 9,866	$ 196,429		5.02%	9.33%
Year 19	$ 10,063	$ 203,305		4.95%	9.52%
Year 20	$ 10,264	$ 210,420		4.88%	9.71%

104

Property Equity - 20 year Projection

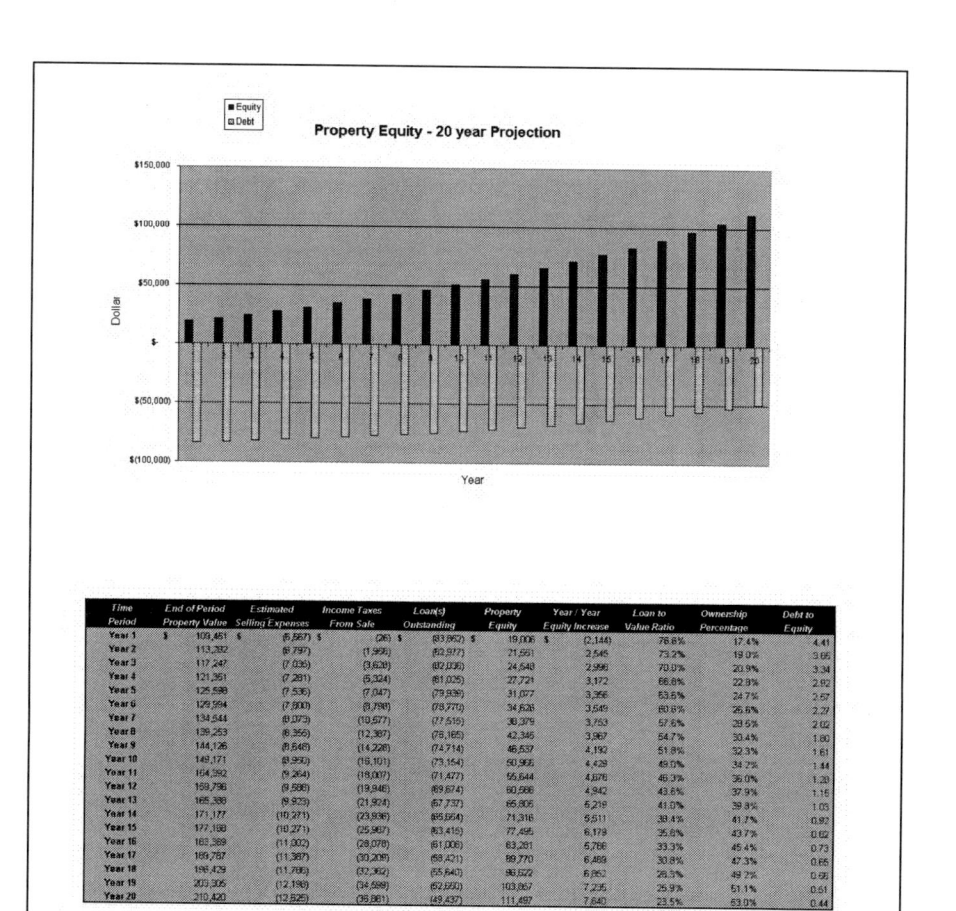

Legend: ■ Equity ☐ Debt

Time Period	End of Period Property Value	Estimated Selling Expenses	Income Taxes From Sale	Loan(s) Outstanding	Property Equity	Year / Year Equity Increase	Loan to Value Ratio	Ownership Percentage	Debt to Equity
Year 1	$ 109,461	$ (6,567)	$ (26)	$ (83,862)	$ 19,006	$ (2,144)	76.8%	17.4%	4.41
Year 2	113,392	(6,797)	(1,956)	(82,977)	21,661	2,545	73.2%	19.0%	3.85
Year 3	117,247	(7,035)	(3,628)	(82,036)	24,548	2,996	70.0%	20.9%	3.34
Year 4	121,361	(7,281)	(5,324)	(81,025)	27,721	3,172	66.8%	22.8%	2.92
Year 5	125,598	(7,536)	(7,047)	(79,936)	31,077	3,356	63.6%	24.7%	2.57
Year 6	129,994	(7,800)	(8,798)	(78,770)	34,626	3,549	60.6%	26.6%	2.27
Year 7	134,544	(8,073)	(10,577)	(77,515)	38,379	3,753	57.6%	28.5%	2.02
Year 8	139,253	(8,355)	(12,387)	(76,165)	42,346	3,967	54.7%	30.4%	1.80
Year 9	144,126	(8,648)	(14,228)	(74,714)	46,537	4,192	51.8%	32.3%	1.61
Year 10	149,171	(8,950)	(16,101)	(73,154)	50,966	4,429	49.0%	34.2%	1.44
Year 11	154,392	(9,264)	(18,007)	(71,477)	55,644	4,676	46.3%	36.0%	1.28
Year 12	159,796	(9,586)	(19,946)	(69,674)	60,586	4,942	43.6%	37.9%	1.15
Year 13	165,388	(9,923)	(21,924)	(67,737)	65,805	5,218	41.0%	39.8%	1.03
Year 14	171,177	(10,271)	(23,936)	(65,654)	71,316	5,511	38.4%	41.7%	0.92
Year 15	177,168	(10,271)	(25,987)	(63,415)	77,495	6,179	35.8%	43.7%	0.82
Year 16	183,369	(11,002)	(28,078)	(61,008)	83,281	5,786	33.3%	45.4%	0.73
Year 17	189,787	(11,387)	(30,208)	(58,421)	89,770	6,489	30.8%	47.3%	0.65
Year 18	196,429	(11,786)	(32,362)	(55,640)	96,622	6,852	28.3%	49.2%	0.58
Year 19	203,305	(12,198)	(34,588)	(52,660)	103,857	7,235	25.9%	51.1%	0.51
Year 20	210,420	(12,625)	(36,861)	(49,437)	111,497	7,640	23.5%	53.0%	0.44

105

Debt Coverage Ratio

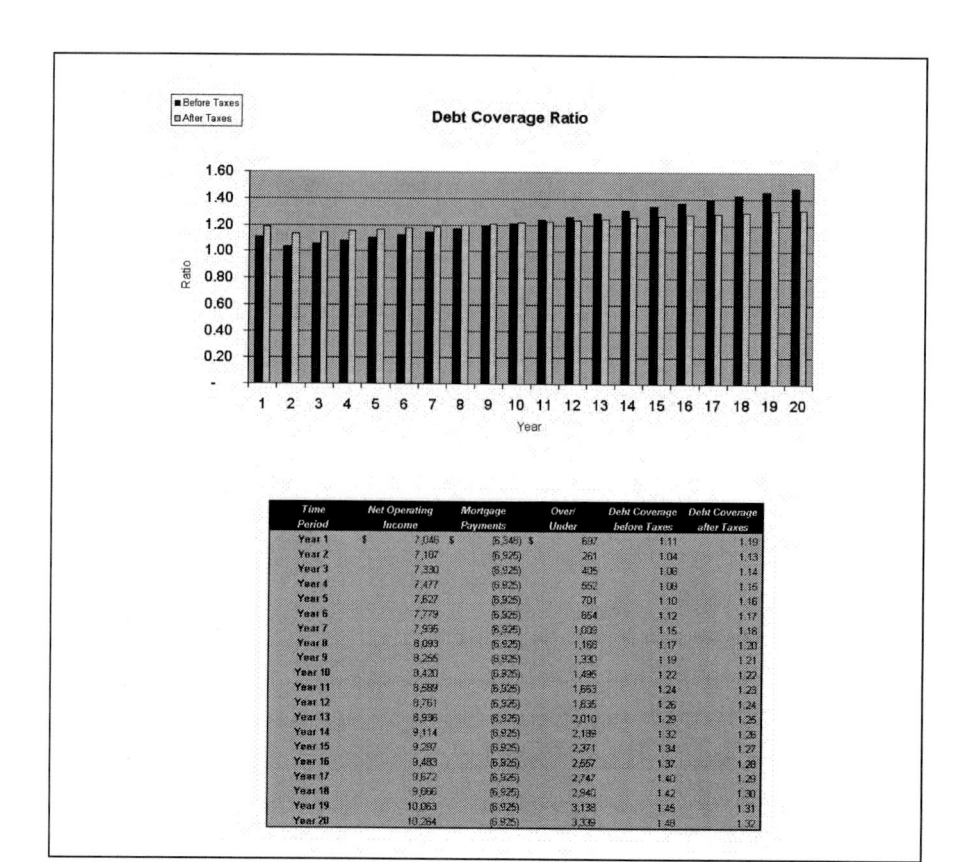

Legend: ■ Before Taxes ☐ After Taxes

Time Period	Net Operating Income	Mortgage Payments	Over/ Under	Debt Coverage before Taxes	Debt Coverage after Taxes
Year 1	$ 7,045	$ (6,348)	$ 697	1.11	1.19
Year 2	7,187	(6,925)	261	1.04	1.13
Year 3	7,330	(6,925)	405	1.06	1.14
Year 4	7,477	(6,925)	552	1.08	1.15
Year 5	7,627	(6,925)	701	1.10	1.16
Year 6	7,779	(6,925)	854	1.12	1.17
Year 7	7,935	(6,925)	1,009	1.15	1.18
Year 8	8,093	(6,925)	1,168	1.17	1.20
Year 9	8,255	(6,925)	1,330	1.19	1.21
Year 10	8,420	(6,925)	1,495	1.22	1.22
Year 11	8,589	(6,925)	1,663	1.24	1.23
Year 12	8,761	(6,925)	1,835	1.26	1.24
Year 13	8,936	(6,925)	2,010	1.29	1.25
Year 14	9,114	(6,925)	2,189	1.32	1.26
Year 15	9,297	(6,925)	2,371	1.34	1.27
Year 16	9,483	(6,925)	2,557	1.37	1.28
Year 17	9,672	(6,925)	2,747	1.40	1.29
Year 18	9,866	(6,925)	2,940	1.42	1.30
Year 19	10,063	(6,925)	3,138	1.45	1.31
Year 20	10,264	(6,925)	3,339	1.48	1.32

Internal Rate of Return

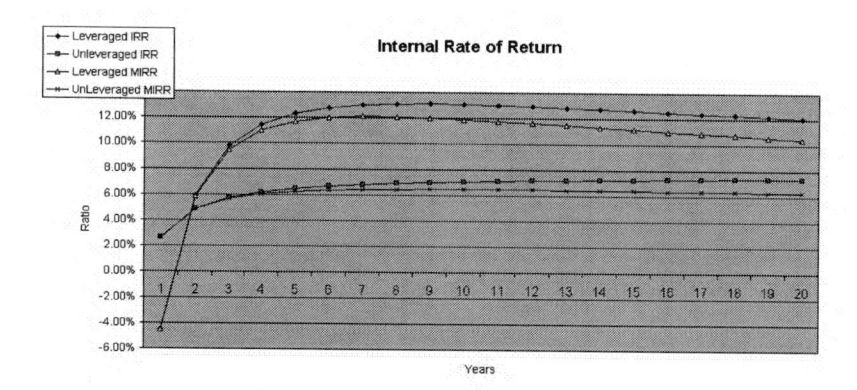

- Leveraged IRR
- Unleveraged IRR
- Leveraged MIRR
- UnLeveraged MIRR

Time Period	Net Cash Flow Plus Refi Proceeds	Cash Flow from Sale	Cumulative Leveraged IRR	Cumulative Unleveraged IRR	Cumulative Leveraged MIRR	Cumulative Unleveraged MIRR
Initial Investment	(21,150)					
Year 1	$ 1,195	$ 19,006	-4.49%	2.65%	-4.49%	2.65%
Year 2	903	21,651	5.90%	4.86%	5.85%	4.66%
Year 3	979	24,548	9.75%	5.75%	9.49%	5.66%
Year 4	1,063	27,721	11.46%	6.19%	11.00%	6.03%
Year 5	1,128	31,077	12.32%	6.46%	11.70%	6.23%
Year 6	1,203	34,626	12.76%	6.65%	12.00%	6.34%
Year 7	1,279	38,379	12.99%	6.79%	12.11%	6.41%
Year 8	1,354	42,345	13.08%	6.89%	12.10%	6.45%
Year 9	1,429	46,537	13.10%	6.98%	12.03%	6.46%
Year 10	1,504	50,966	13.07%	7.05%	11.92%	6.47%
Year 11	1,579	55,644	13.01%	7.10%	11.78%	6.47%
Year 12	1,652	60,586	12.93%	7.15%	11.64%	6.46%
Year 13	1,725	65,805	12.84%	7.19%	11.49%	6.44%
Year 14	1,796	71,316	12.74%	7.23%	11.34%	6.42%
Year 15	1,867	77,136	12.63%	7.26%	11.18%	6.40%
Year 16	1,936	83,281	12.52%	7.28%	11.04%	6.38%
Year 17	2,004	89,770	12.41%	7.31%	10.89%	6.36%
Year 18	2,069	96,622	12.31%	7.33%	10.75%	6.33%
Year 19	2,133	103,857	12.20%	7.35%	10.61%	6.31%
Year 20	2,194	111,497	12.10%	7.36%	10.47%	6.28%

Summary Cash Flow

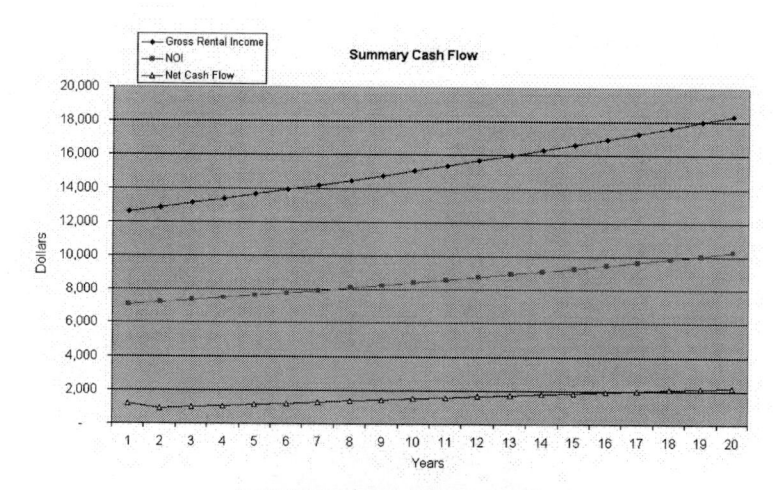

Time Period	Gross Rental Income	Net Operating Income	Net Cash Flow
Year 1	12,600	7,046	1,195
Year 2	12,852	7,187	903
Year 3	13,109	7,330	976
Year 4	13,371	7,477	1,053
Year 5	13,639	7,627	1,128
Year 6	13,911	7,779	1,203
Year 7	14,190	7,935	1,279
Year 8	14,473	8,093	1,354
Year 9	14,763	8,255	1,429
Year 10	15,058	8,420	1,504
Year 11	15,359	8,589	1,578
Year 12	15,667	8,761	1,652
Year 13	15,980	8,936	1,725
Year 14	16,299	9,114	1,796
Year 15	16,625	9,297	1,867
Year 16	16,958	9,483	1,936
Year 17	17,297	9,672	2,004
Year 18	17,643	9,866	2,069
Year 19	17,996	10,063	2,133
Year 20	18,356	10,264	2,194

Appendix 2: Input Data Sheet for Sample Analysis #2

Input Data Screen

Property Name: Sample Analysis #2
Case Description:
Address:
Address:

[Sensitivity Analysis] [Executive Report]
[Main Report] [User Guide]
[Graphs & Reports] [APOD Report]

I. Rental Income & Expenses

Rental Income / Rent Roll:	[Enter Rent Roll]
Operating Expenses:	[Enter Expenses]
Enter Average Vacancy Rate:	4.20%
Annual Rental Income Growth Rate (%) [Enter Annual Rates] Apply This Rate Every Year =>	2.00%
Annual Operating Expense Increase (%):	2.00%

II. Property Costs & Characteristics

Select Residential, Commercial Property or Raw Land		Single-Family
Number of Units / Total Square Footage of Property	1	1,500

Purchase Price of Rental Property:		
Contract Purchase Price	$	105,000
Initial Improvements	$	-
Closing Costs	$	750
Other Initial Costs		-
Enter 5-Year Personal Property =>	$	-
% of Cost Allocated to Land	20.00%	$ 105,750 <== Total Cost

Current Fair Market Value (FMV) of Rental Property:	$	105,750
Annual Appreciation Rate (%): [Enter Annual Rates] Apply This Rate Every Year --->		3.50%
Future Selling Expenses (as a % of Selling Price):		6.00%

	Description	Amount	Select Year Improvement to be Made	Will the improvement increase the property's FMV?
Future Property Improvements	Improvement	$ 5,000	1	No
		$ -	2	No
		$ -	2	No
	Total	$ 5,000		

III. Financing [Amort Schedules]

	Mortgage #1	Mortgage #2	Mortgage #3
Amount Borrowed or Assumed:	$ 84,600	$ -	$ -
Interest Rate:	7.250%	[Enter Loan Rate]	[Enter Loan Rate]
Interest Only?	No	No	No
Enter Start Month of the Loan:	Month 1	Month 1	Month 1
Enter Start Year of the Loan:	Year 1	Year 1	Year 1
Term / Remaining Term of Loan (In Months):	360	360	360
Is this to Refinance Mortgage #1 or #2	n/a	No - New Loan	No - New Loan
Additional Monthly Principal Payments	-	-	-
Monthly Mortgage Payment: (Formula)	$ 577.12	$ -	$ -
Loan Origination Points	-	-	
Loan Origination Points (In Dollars)	$ -	$ -	$ -

Initial Investment or Down Payment (Cost less Debt - Automatically Calculated)	$ 21,150
Down Payment as a Percent of Fair Market Value	20.0%
Down Payment as a Percent of Cost	20.0%

IV. Income Taxes

Federal Marginal Income Tax Rate:	28.0%
Federal Long-Term Capital Gains Rate:	15%
State Marginal Income Tax Rate:	5%
Are Your Losses Limited by the Passive Loss Rules?	No
Like-Kind Exchange on Disposition?	No

Appendix 3: Input Data Sheet for Sample Analysis #3

Input Data Screen

Property Name: Sample Analysis #3
Case Description:
Address:
Address:

I. Rental Income & Expenses

Rental Income / Rent Roll:	[Enter Rent Roll]
Operating Expenses:	[Enter Expenses]
Enter Average Vacancy Rate:	0.00%
Annual Rental Income Growth Rate (%) [Enter Annual Rates] Apply This Rate Every Year =>	2.00%
Annual Operating Expense Increase (%):	2.00%

II. Property Costs & Characteristics

Select Residential, Commercial Property or Raw Land	Single-Family
Number of Units / Total Square Footage of Property	

Purchase Price of Rental Property:		
Contract Purchase Price	$	550,000
Initial Improvements	$	12,000
Closing Costs	$	1,750
Other Initial Costs		-
Other Initial Costs		-
Enter 5-Year Personal Property =>	$	-
% of Cost Allocated to Land	20.00%	$ 563,750 <== Total Cost

Current Fair Market Value (FMV) of Rental Property:	$ 650,000
Annual Appreciation Rate (%): [Enter Annual Rates] Apply This Rate Every Year ==>	8.00%
Future Selling Expenses (as a % of Selling Price):	6.00%

Future Property Improvements	Description	Amount	Select Year Improvement to be Made	Will the improvement increase the property's FMV?
		$ -	4	No
		$ -	2	No
		$ -	2	No
		$ -	2	No
		$ -	2	No
		$ -	2	No
	Total	$ -		

III. Financing [Amort Schedules]

	Mortgage #1	Mortgage #2	Mortgage #3
Amount Borrowed or Assumed:	$ 451,000	$ -	$ -
Interest Rate:	8.000%	[Enter Loan Rate]	[Enter Loan Rate]
Interest Only?	Yes	No	No
Enter Start Month of the Loan:	Month 1	Month 1	Month 1
Enter Start Year of the Loan:	Year 1	Year 1	Year 1
Term / Remaining Term of Loan (In Months):	360	360	360
Is this to Refinance Mortgage #1 or #2	n/a	No - New Loan	No - New Loan
Additional Monthly Principal Payments	-	-	-
Monthly Mortgage Payment: (Formula)	$ 3,006.67	$ -	$ -
Loan Origination Points	-	-	
Loan Origination Points (In Dollars):	$ -	$ -	$ -

Negative Amortization Option

Negative Amortization Payment	$ -	$ -
Override Payment Calculated Above?	No	No

Initial Investment or Down Payment (Cost less Debt - Automatically Calculated)	$ 112,750
Down Payment as a Percent of Fair Market Value	17.3%
Down Payment as a Percent of Cost	20.0%

IV. Income Taxes

Federal Marginal Income Tax Rate:	28.0%
Federal Long-Term Capital Gains Rate:	15%
State Marginal Income Tax Rate:	5%
Are Your Losses Limited by the Passive Loss Rules?	Yes
Like-Kind Exchange on Disposition?	No

Appendix 4 Input Data Sheet for Sample Analysis #4

Input Data Screen

Property Name:	Sample Analysis #4
Case Description:	
Address:	
Address:	

[Sensitivity Analysis] [Executive Report]
[Main Report] [User Guide]
[Graphs & Reports] [APOD Report]

I. Rental Income & Expenses

Rental Income / Rent Roll:	[Enter Rent Roll]
Operating Expenses:	[Enter Expenses]
Enter Average Vacancy Rate:	8.00%
Annual Rental Income Growth Rate (%) [Enter Annual Rates] Apply This Rate Every Year =>	0.00%
Annual Operating Expense Increase (%):	1.00%

II. Property Costs & Characteristics

Select Residential, Commercial Property or Raw Land		Office Building
Number of Units / Total Square Footage of Property	5	4,500

Purchase Price of Rental Property:		
Contract Purchase Price	$	455,000
Initial Improvements		
Closing Costs	$	10,000
Other Initial Costs		-
Other Initial Costs		-
Enter 5-Year Personal Property =>	$	
% of Cost Allocated to Land	20.00%	$ 465,000 <== Total Cost

Current Fair Market Value (FMV) of Rental Property:
Annual Appreciation Rate (%): [Enter Annual Rates] Use as Cap Rate to Value Property ==> 7.50%
Future Selling Expenses (as a % of Selling Price): 6.00%

	Description	Amount	Select Year Improvement to be Made	Will the improvement increase the property's FMV?
Future Property Improvements		$ -	4	No
		$ -	2	No
		$ -	2	No
	Total	$ -		

III. Financing [Amort Schedules]

	Mortgage #1	Mortgage #2	Mortgage #3
Amount **Borrowed** or **Assumed**	$ 372,000	$ -	$ -
Interest **Rate**	8.500%	[Enter Loan Rate]	[Enter Loan Rate]
Interest Only?	No	No	No
Enter **Start Month** of the Loan:	Month 1	Month 1	Month 1
Enter **Start Year** of the Loan:	Year 1	Year 1	Year 1
Term / Remaining Term of Loan (**In Months**):	360	360	360
Is this to Refinance Mortgage #1 or #2	n/a	No - New Loan	No - New Loan
Additional Monthly Principal Payments	-	-	-
Monthly Mortgage Payment: (Formula)	$ 2,860.36	$ -	$ -
Loan Origination **Points**	-	-	-
Loan Origination Points (In Dollars)	$ -	$ -	$ -

Initial Investment or Down Payment (Cost less Debt - Automatically Calculated)	$	93,000
Down Payment as a Percent of Fair Market Value		0.0%
Down Payment as a Percent of Cost		20.0%

IV. Income Taxes

Federal Marginal Income Tax Rate:	28.0%
Federal Long-Term Capital Gains Rate:	15%
State Marginal Income Tax Rate:	5%
Are Your Losses Limited by the Passive Loss Rules?	No
Like-Kind Exchange on Disposition?	No

Rental Income / Rent Roll
Sample Analysis #4

Enter Lease Description	Monthly Rent	Vacant / Incentive Months in the First Year
Unit 1	$ 1,250	0
Unit 2	$ 1,250	0
Unit 3	$ 1,250	0
Unit 4	$ 1,250	0
Unit 5	$ 1,250	0
Unit 6	$ -	0
Unit 7	$ -	0
Unit 8	$ -	0
Unit 9	$ -	0
Unit 10	$ -	0
Unit 11	$ -	0
Unit 12	$ -	0
Unit 13	$ -	0
Unit 14	$ -	0

Total Gross Monthly Income $ 6,250

Estimated Annual Income 75,000
Estimated Annual Vacancy: $ 6,000

Other Monthly Income:

Description	Amount	Growth Rate
Laundry	$ -	0.00%
Late Fees	$ -	0.00%
Parking	$ -	0.00%
Mainten	$ -	0.00%
Other	$ -	0.00%
Total	-	

Annual Rental Expense Input Screen

Total Annual Expenses:	$ 28,770	(from below)	
Annual Increase	1.00%	(from Input Screen)	
Monthly Expenses	$ 2,398	$ -	

Expense Description	Annual Amount	Percentage of Total	Percentage of Revenue
Accounting	$ -	0.00%	0.00%
Advertising	$ -	0.00%	0.00%
Association Fees		0.00%	0.00%
Auto & Travel	$ -	0.00%	0.00%
Cleaning	$ -	0.00%	0.00%
Commissions	$ -	0.00%	0.00%
Insurance	$ 4,950	17.21%	6.60%
Lawn Maintenance	$ 5,400	18.77%	7.20%
Legal	$ -	0.00%	0.00%
Maintenance	$ 3,500	12.17%	4.67%
Other	$ -	0.00%	0.00%
Payroll	$ -	0.00%	0.00%
Professional Fees	$ -	0.00%	0.00%
Repairs	$ -	0.00%	0.00%
Supplies	$ -	0.00%	0.00%
Taxes:			0.00%
Property Taxes	$ 8,425	29.28%	11.23%
Personal Property	$ -	0.00%	0.00%
Payroll	$ -	0.00%	0.00%
Other	$ -	0.00%	0.00%
Trash Removal	$ -	0.00%	0.00%
Utilities:			0.00%
Electricity	$ 3,600	12.51%	4.80%
Water	$ 2,895	10.06%	3.86%
Gas	$ -	0.00%	0.00%
Telephone	$ -	0.00%	0.00%
Other Utilities	$ -	0.00%	0.00%
Miscellaneous	$ -	0.00%	0.00%
Miscellaneous	$ -	0.00%	0.00%
Miscellaneous	$ -	0.00%	0.00%
Miscellaneous	$ -	0.00%	0.00%
Miscellaneous	$ -	0.00%	0.00%
Total Annual Expenses	**$ 28,770**		

Annual Property Operating Data (APOD)

		Year 3	$/Sq ft	Year 4	$/Sq ft	Year 5	$/Sq ft
Rental Income							
Gross Rental Income	$	75,000	16.67	75,000	16.67	75,000	16.67
Other Income		-		-		-	
Vacancy & Credits		(6,000)	(1.33)	(6,000)	(1.33)	(6,000)	(1.33)
Management Fees (if any)		-		-		-	
Total Net Rental Income	$	69,000	15.33	69,000	15.33	69,000	15.33
Rental Expenses							
Accounting	$	-	-	-	-	-	-
Advertising		-	-	-	-	-	-
Association Fees		-	-	-	-	-	-
Auto & Travel		-	-	-	-	-	-
Cleaning		-	-	-	-	-	-
Commissions		-	-	-	-	-	-
Insurance		5,049	1.12	5,100	1.13	5,151	1.14
Lawn Maintenance		5,509	1.22	5,564	1.24	5,619	1.25
Legal		-		-		-	
Maintenance		3,570	0.79	3,606	0.80	3,642	0.81
Other		-	-	-	-	-	-
Payroll		-	-	-	-	-	-
Professional Fees		-	-	-	-	-	-
Repairs		-	-	-	-	-	-
Supplies		-	-	-	-	-	-
Taxes:							
Property Taxes		8,594	1.91	8,680	1.93	8,767	1.95
Personal Property		-	-	-	-	-	-
Payroll		-	-	-	-	-	-
Other		-	-	-	-	-	-
Trash Removal		-	-	-	-	-	-
Utilities:							
Electricity		3,672	0.82	3,709	0.82	3,746	0.83
Water		2,953	0.66	2,983	0.66	3,013	0.67
Gas		-	-	-	-	-	-
Telephone		-	-	-	-	-	-
Other Utilities		-	-	-	-	-	-
Miscellaneous		-	-	-	-	-	-
Miscellaneous		-	-	-	-	-	-
Miscellaneous		-	-	-	-	-	-
Miscellaneous		-	-	-	-	-	-
Miscellaneous		-	-	-	-	-	-
One-Time Expenses:		-	-	-	-	-	-
Total Expenses	$	29,348	6.52	29,642	6.59	29,938	6.65
Net Rental Operating Income	$	39,652	8.81	39,358	8.75	39,062	8.68

Appendix 5 - 2007 Individual Tax Tables

Single

If taxable income is over--	But not over-	The tax is:
$0	$7,825	10% of the amount over $0
$7,825	$31,850	$782.50 plus 15% of the amount over 7,825
$31,850	$77,100	$4,386.25 plus 25% of the amount over 31,850
$77,100	$160,850	$15,698.75 plus 28% of the amount over 77,100
$160,850	$349,700	$39,148.75 plus 33% of the amount over 160,850
$349,700	no limit	$101,469.25 plus 35% of the amount over 349,700

Married Filing Jointly or Qualifying Widow(er)

If taxable income is over--	But not over-	The tax is:
$0	$15,650	10% of the amount over $0
$15,650	$63,700	$1,565.00 plus 15% of the amount over 15,650
$63,700	$128,500	$8,772.50 plus 25% of the amount over 63,700
$128,500	$195,850	$24,972.50 plus 28% of the amount over 128,500
$195,850	$349,700	$43,830.50 plus 33% of the amount over 195,850
$349,700	no limit	$94,601.00 plus 35% of the amount over 349,700

Married Filing Separately

If taxable income is over--	But not over--	The tax is:
$0	$7,825	10% of the amount over $0
$7,825	$31,850	$782.50 plus 15% of the amount over 7,825
$31,850	$64,250	$4,386.25 plus 25% of the amount over 31,850
$64,250	$97,925	$12,486.25 plus 28% of the amount over

If taxable income is over--	But not over--	The tax is:
		64,250
$97,925	$174,850	$21,915.25 plus 33% of the amount over 97,925
$174,850	no limit	$47,300.50 plus 35% of the amount over 174,850

Head of Household

If taxable income is over--	But not over--	The tax is:
$0	$11,200	10% of the amount over $0
$11,200	$42,650	$1,120.00 plus 15% of the amount over 11,200
$42,650	$110,100	$5,837.50 plus 25% of the amount over 42,650
$110,100	$178,350	$22,700.00 plus 28% of the amount over 110,100
$178,350	$349,700	$41,810.00 plus 33% of the amount over 178,550
$349,700	no limit	$98,355.50 plus 35% of the amount over 349,700

2007 Long-Term Capital Gain Tax Rates:

For taxpayers in the 10% or 15% bracket -- **5%**

For taxpayers in higher brackets -- **15%**

Tax on unrecaptured Sec. 1250 gain -- **25%**